ESSAYS ON THE HISTORY OF UKRAINE

(second edition)

Summit-book
2023

UDC 821.111(477)'06-4-94(02.034)
    C50

Smeshko, Ihor
C50   Essays on the history of Ukraine / Ihor Smeshko. – Kyiv: Sum-
    mit-book, 2023

        ISBN 978-966-986-607-3

        What is the building of modern European civilization? On what foun-
    dation is it built? And the main thing: were the components of this civiliza-
    tion present - from the most ancient times! — on the territory of modern
    Ukraine? This complex of issues is analysed in this essay.
                                            UDC 821.111(477)'06-4-94(02.034)

Popular Science Edition

Smeshko Ihor
Essays on the History of Ukraine

Responsible for the issue: Mariia Rotarchuk
Printing Director: Andrii Bodeichuk
Publishing House Director: Ivan Stepurin

"SAMIT KNYHA" Publishing House
Ukraine, Kyiv, 25 Observatorna Street
Tel. (063) 757-74-80. sbook.com.ua, sinbook@ukr.net
Publishing certificate DK 5335 dated 20.04.2017

ISBN 978-966-986-607-3

CONTENTS

About the author

Ihor Smeshko – Officer, Scientist and Statesman. Colonel-General in Armed Forces of Ukraine; Doctor of Technical Science and Professor of System Analyses; Ukraine's Laureate award recipient in Science and Technology; Ambassador Extraordinary and Plenipotentiary of Ukraine.

Former: Professor at the Kyiv Army Air Defense Academy; Executive Secretary of the Expert Scientific Committee of Ukraine's Ministry of Defence (MOD); Defence Attaché to the USA; Chairman of Ukraine's Joint Intelligence Committee; Chairman of MOD's Main Intelligence Directorate; Defence Attaché to Switzerland; Permanent Ukrainian MOD's Representative to International Organizations in Geneva; Chairman of the Military-Technical Cooperation Policy Committee; Chairman of Ukraine's Security Service; Acting Secretary of the National Security and Defence Council.

(More detailed: V. A. Smelov "Ihor Smeshko. Unfinished dossier of secret service general..."/ V. A. Smelov – K.: Summit Book, 2012. – 568 p.)

Link to download: *https://sylaichest.org/wp-content/uploads/2019/06/dossier_ukr.pdf.*

Review

'If you don't know where you are coming from, you don't know where you are going, because you don't know where you are'. This simple wisdom does not only apply to geography, but also to history and none the least to our value system. At a time when we are increasingly dealing with the 'Centre of Europe' and the future of our continent, it is of the greatest importance to develop an understanding for our past. Also to be able to navigate our way through all the misinformation and 'fake news' we are bombarded with all the time.

Ukraine has unjustly been far too transparent on our maps in the past. Many of us were not aware of its diverse, rich and independent history, its huge natural and human resources, its defining role in the formation of the European continent.

I'm very grateful to Ihor Smeshko for his Essays, drawing an important picture of Ukraine and the surrounding states, for a better understanding of today's war. He draws not only from the deep knowledge of a historian, but also from the very hands-on experience as a soldier and diplomat. Gen. Smeshko moves Ukraine from being an Eastern border state of Europe to taking a central role for the future of our continent.

**Archduke
Karl Habsburg-Lotharingen**

Review

"*General Smeshko, through meticulous historical research, has unlocked Russia's closely guarded state secrets that – even now – are being played out on Ukraine's bloody battlefields. When Putin ordered his armies into Ukraine he intended to solve the Kremlin's 400-year old «Ukrainian problem» by annihilating Europe's second largest nation.*

Smeshko's extensively documented «Essays» expose many of the lies and reasons why western Kremlinologists and «Russian studies» academicians have been so mistaken in their understanding of Russia's implacable threat to democracy and western civilization. The author weaves together three millenia of history of the land we now know as Ukraine by providing fascinating and little known insights and facts that support his underlying theme that Ukrainians are not now and never were part of «russkiy mir».

Learned why the USSR banned one of Karl Marx's books; why czar Peter I engaged in identity theft 300 years ago by changing his empire's name from «Moscovia» to «Russia»; why Putin built a huge monument to Prince Volodymyr of Kyiv-Rus to justify his invasion of Crimea; how the development of European civilization from as early as the Hellenic era encompassed the territory of Ukraine; and, how, contrary to Putin's «one people» myth, Ukraine and Russia developed along very disparate cultural, linguistic, juridical, and institutional vectors; and much, much more.....

Although not always an easy read, I highly recommend «Essays» to all who seek a better understanding of today»s headlines".

Hon. George Woloshyn, MBA, JD
Former Associate Director of U.S OPM and FEMA,
Inspector General of a Bank Regulatory Agency

Preface

What constitutes the edifice of modern European civilization? What is its foundation? And (most importantly) were building bricks of this civilization present in the territory of contemporary Ukraine since antiquity?

The history of mankind has proven that it is the national idea, which reflects the historical experience of a particular nation and its uniqueness among other nations, determines the mission of its existence. It essentially represents the formalized self-awareness,

It is noteworthy that—unlike any other post-Soviet republic (the Baltic states included) — only the territory of what is now Ukraine was home to permanent Roman garrisons (in Olbia, Chersonesus, and Tyras) from the late 1ˢᵗ century BC to the 4ᵗʰ century AD. In particular, cohorts of the 1ˢᵗ Italian, 2ⁿᵈ Herculean, 11ᵗʰ Claudian, and 5ᵗʰ Macedonian legions were stationed for a long time in Chersonesus (photo courtesy of Andriy Krymsky).

purpose, and meaning of the existence of any successful nation. It ideologically creates programmatic prerequisites for its further progressive development among other peoples of the world.

Scholars in search of a modern national "idea" of Ukraine should proceed from the premise that this "idea" has to include the core spiritual and material underpinnings vital in the building of modern Ukrainian institutions of government, law, and civil society.

But first we must identify the essential elements of present day Ukraine and the main attributes of contemporary Ukrainians. Are they Europeans or Eurasians in terms of their origin, culture, and striving for continued progression? Do they have certain spiritual values that have survived intact across all stages of their historical evolution? Such values could lay the groundwork for their continued evolvement.

For starters, let us define the actual structure – the "edifice" – of modern European civilization. This edifice was erected atop a foundation comprised of three core components: the first one is the philosophy and culture of ancient Greece; the second one is the theory and practice of government and law of ancient Rome; and the third one is Christian morals and religion.

The walls of this edifice were built using the products and ideals extant at various stages of its evolution, including: the Renaissance in Italy and France; the Reformation in Germany and other west European countries; the doctrines of Humanism and the French Revolution; and the legal principles of the Byzantine Code of Justinian, Britain's Magna Carta, the Ruska Pravda of Kyiv's Yaroslav the Wise, Germany's Magdeburg Law, and the Napoleonic Civil Code. This process was also largely impacted by the great geographical discoveries in the New World.

The roof of this edifice, as we know it today, was crafted by the European bourgeois revolutions in the mid-19th century, the 1917 October Revolution in Russia, the two World Wars of the 20th century, and the recent Cold War between East and West.

The process by which this civilization was constructed had been constantly in dialectic unity and opposition with other (often essentially dissimilar) civilizations of the world. Without their active impact on its evolution and historical development, European civilization would not have become what it currently is. In order to comprehend the role that Ukraine played in all of those processes, we need to first delve into the depth of centuries and trace the history and evolution of the tribes, races, and societies that had previously inhabited the territory of what is now Ukraine.

Our quest begins more than 7,000 years ago in the heartland of Europe on land which is now home to a people known as "Ukrainians" and who are, in greater part, descendants of the various residents who had previously, for various periods, occupied or passed through their land. As we move through time and space we look for evidence of societies and communities that may have either left vestiges of their civilization for later generations and settlers, or had been influenced by those later generations or settlers.

European civilization and historical traces of its foundation in the territory of contemporary Ukraine

The earliest known civilization that flourished in Europe (between the 6th and 3rd millennia BC, even before the great civilizations of Egypt and Mesopotamia) was that of the enigmatic Trypilians who settled an area stretching from the Balkans and across much of Ukraine. They built the earliest known cities which may be the key to understanding how European civilization emerged from the Stone Age. The Trypilians – in a pattern common throughout Europe – assimilated the culture of pre-existing tribes while advancing European civilization by urbanization, agricultural enhancements, and egalitarian social structures.

Between the 1st millennium BC and the 8th century AD, such ethnic groups as the Cimmerians, Scythians, Taurians, Sarmatians, ancient Greeks and Romans, Goths, and Huns, and, more recently,

Map of Scythian Lands c.500 BC
https://www.historyfiles.co.uk/FeaturesEurope/EuropeMap500BC.htm

Ancient Greek colonies in the northern Black Sea region
https://commons.wikimedia.org/wiki/File:Ancient_Greek_Colonies_of_N_Black_Sea.
png?uselang=uk

Slavs and Vikings left their noticeable traces and shaped the history of the land we now know as Ukraine.

Ancient Greeks and eventually Romans refer to them in their historical treatises as Scythia, Sarmatia, and, in the 3rd – 4th centuries AD, Gothia. It was also here that a powerful Slavic state, "Kyivan Rus," ruled wide territories of Eastern Europe in the 9th – 13th centuries AD and is considered the "cradle" of modern Ukraine. Having served the purpose of defending a very vulnerable and divided Europe for centuries from numerous invading nomadic tribes, Kyivan Rus finally succumbed to the Mongol hordes of Genghis Khan.

An unearthed residential quarter in the city of Olbia (the center of the eponymous Greek colony) on the right bank of the Buh Estuary near the village of Parutyne, Ochakiv District

Assuming that the culture of ancient Greece (8th to 2nd

centuries BC) and ancient Rome (5ᵗʰ century BC to 5ᵗʰ century AD) as well as Christian morals and religion are the three components underlying European civilization, it is a historical fact that all three were among the first in Europe to appear in the territory of what is now Ukraine. Unlike Britain and Germany as well as many other west European nations that had never been part of the "Hellenic World," the territory of Ukraine was home to numerous Greek colonies that were organically integrated into Hellenic civilization as early as 6ᵗʰ century BC.

It is also a historical fact that in those ancient times (5ᵗʰ – 1ˢᵗ centuries BC) when only patriarchal cultures of splintered barbarian clans ruled in most of northwestern Europe, the ideas of Plato, Aristotle, and Demosthenes were already known and spreading in parts of Ukraine, just as in the Greek colonies of Italy, France, and Spain. Theaters were already playing the tragedies of Aeschylus and Sophocles and comedies of Euripides. The inter-mingling, inter-marriage, and trade between Greeks and local residents exposed the native population to Homer's *Iliad* and *Odyssey*, and early forms of democratic governance and constitutions as practiced in small city states.

In order to understand what kind of culture and philosophy had influence over the residents of at least some of the territory of contemporary Ukraine, and which specific features would eventually manifest themselves in Ukrainians of the Cossack era, here is what one famous historian wrote in the *History of Mankind*, a collective work of German historians:

"Hardly any other people had been so luckily and richly endowed by nature and God as had been the ancient Greeks. Open to merriment and enjoyment, having a loving fondness of singing, dancing, and gymnastic exercises, the Greeks all the while had an unclouded and insightful understanding of nature and its phenomena, a vibrant striving for knowledge, and an inquisitive mind that – while being a far cry from the abstruse reasoning of Egyptians or Indian sages – bravely searched for knowledge about the nature of things through observation. They were also blessed with an overpowering desire for companionship and a subtle appreciation of the beauty of shapes.

"This sense of all things beautiful, which we haven't encountered in any other of the ancient peoples, is a hallmark of the Greeks and a priori puts them a few rungs above all other peoples. The Greeks highly valued the appearance, the beauty of stature, the decorum of movements even in happiness or sorrow, the melodiousness of speech, restraint in expressions, and unaffected dignity in communication; this attitude towards appearance is reflected in the ancient Greek expression καλος καγαθος that can be best translated as 'without beauty, there is no virtue'...

"Greek 'cult' of all things beautiful, which has not flourished as fully anywhere else, left an imprint on national poetry, music, fine art and sculpture, much like on philosophy and science... The Greek's unprecedented freedom and multifaceted development of a separate individual were closely intertwined with these philosophical trends.

"The Greeks were also physically fit and famous for their courage on the battlefield, cunning, modesty in relationships, and adeptness at various technical arts... Hence they viewed all non-Hellenics as barbarians. Yet this arrogance was unlike the blunt indifference of the Egyptians, and nothing like the ardent religious hatred of the Hebrews for all things foreign. It manifested itself through friendly humour that stemmed from their own self-awareness.

"The Greeks liked to welcome foreigners in order to influence them with their example and relationships. On the other hand, they did not think twice before adopting from foreigners all those things they considered worth imitating. They borrowed astronomical and mathematical knowledge from the Egyptians and the science of shipbuilding, navigation, and mining from the Phoenicians... The Greeks were the first to stop turning the fruits of their research into a national or caste secret, and, instead, willingly shared their findings with the entire world.

"Hellenism is the first historical example of a conquest accomplished not through force or commerce, but through spiritual supe-

riority...It later served as the foundation on which the proud structure of Rome arose ..." [5, p. 20].

Rome became the second most important contributor to the foundation of European civilization. Having absorbed the best achievements in philosophy and culture from the Greeks, Romans excelled in developing principles of sound government. Without Roman law and Rome's experience in public governance, modern European law and the parliamentary system may have looked very different from what they are today.

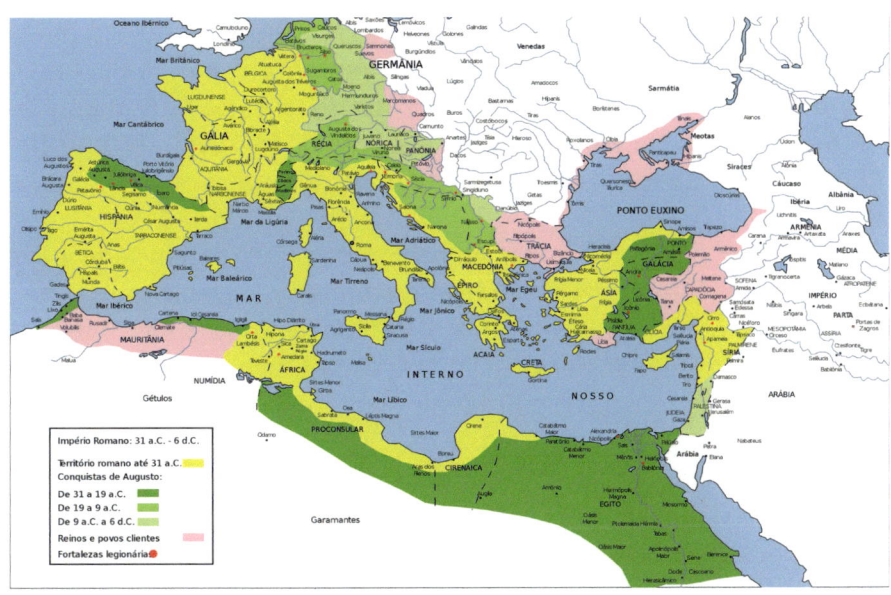

Expansion of the Roman Empire under Augustus (territory as of 31 BC is shown in yellow; conquests in 31-19 BC – in dark green; 19-9 BC – in bright green; 9 BC to 6 AD – in light green; client kingdoms – in pink (source: Wikimedia Commons) https://commons.wikimedia.org/ wiki/File:Imp%C3%A9rioRomano_-_30_a.C.-6_d.C.-pt.svg

The Roman Empire expanded much farther to the west and north of Europe than did the "Hellenic World"of ancient Greece. Its civilizing influence covered the expanses of what are now Italy, France, Spain, Britain, Austria, Switzerland, Hungary, Romania, Bulgaria and parts of Germany.

But in its eastward expansion, the empire extended only as far as the Bosporan kingdom. *(This kingdom, descended from Greek colonies along Ukraine's northern Black Sea region, encompassed much of the southern part of what is now Ukraine.)* It is noteworthy that unlike any other post-Soviet republic only Ukraine hosted permanent Roman garrisons. These included garrisons in Olbia, Chersonesus, and Tyras from the late 1st century BC to the 4th century AD, and cohorts of the 1st Italian, 2nd Herculean, 11th Claudian, and 5th Macedonian legions serving long rotational tours especially in Chersonesus.

In 24 BC Rome helped the former Greek city-state of Chersonesus (now Sevastopol) win its independence from the Bosporan Kingdom. This city became the administrative center of Roman rule in the entire northern Black Sea region, and the home base of the Roman Navy squadron of the Flavian fleet stationed at Mysia in the Black Sea.

So what could these new inhabitants of Ukrainian land have brought with them in the dim and distant past? Even though their influence over the entire territory of contemporary Ukraine was somewhat limited, ancient treasures, such as Roman coins dating to the 2nd century BC are still being discovered in the heart of ancient Kyiv. Roman presence along the Black Sea cost of Ukraine did not fail to leave part of its cultural heritage to Ukraine's ancestors. Once again we quote from the *History of Mankind*:

"The superiority of Rome over the rest of the world, much like the superiority of the ancient Greeks over the eastern part of the Mediterranean Sea was, based on moral principles; and yet the moral concepts of Rome were different in many ways from those of the Greeks, and so their influence was different.

"Rome arose from the idea of the state, from a profound understanding of, and unwavering adherence to, the idea of the state's indivisibility, omnipotence, and grandeur. A native of Rome placed *rem publicum* above all else. He did not perceive himself as a separate individual the way the Greeks did, but merely as an integral building block of the state, and it was only in this way that he had a right to exist. Yet because of this he was brimming with a sense of particular grandeur. The good of the state was the supreme law, and everything else had to be subordinated to it: individuality, ethnicity, culture, and religion.

"The Romans were not intolerant of foreign ethnicity and cultures or foreign faith: rather, they treated all of them with indifference. However, they expected unconditional subordination to the idea of the state from anyone who became a Roman subject. That is why an "independent" individual experienced more restrictive confines compared to the Greeks; for a Roman an individual mattered within a social life that had been permeated with a single common spirit.

"On the upside, the Romans developed an unwavering, robust system of government and an inexhaustible living force that was guided by one multi-headed yet single-voiced will towards continued expansion of the concept of "state". Needless to say, the Roman state also had different political trends and internal strife. Their political ideas and forms of government changed over time with the monarchy transforming into an aristocratic republic; the aristocratic republic evolving into a democracy; and the democracy sliding into an oligarchy and "caesarism." Yet all of this turmoil and changes had one common trait: a sense of the need for the state's unity and omnipotence..." [5, pp. 26–27].

While the then native inhabitants of Ukraine were being exposed to Greek and Roman culture, values, and technical advancements, they were also undergoing internal cultural evolution from new migratory settlers moving into Ukraine, such as the Scythians, who either replaced or intermingled with the earlier occupants. The "Father of History," Herodotus, left the first written historical account (dated 445 BC) of the Cimmerians and Scythians.

The Scythians displaced the Cimmerians in the 6-7th centuries BC. Although migratory and nomadic in their origin they became skilled farmers and chief exporters of grain through the Greek colonies in the 4th-5th centuries BC. During the same period the "Royal Scythians", who were considered to be the ruling tribe among the

The areas inhabited by Scythian tribes (in some maps, Scythian tillers are also referred to as Scolots) and one of the versions of a failed campaign of Darius the Great against Scythians. Source: Wikimedia Commons (https://commons.wikimedia.org/wiki/File:MapU_5.jpg)

Scythians, switched from a nomadic lifestyle to grain cultivation. The Scythians were a free people who could take up arms at any time and defend themselves against any threat. Many of them willingly adopted the superior culture of the Greeks and mixed with them. The best example is the Bosporan Kingdom that was half-Greek and half-Scythian.

Around 513 BC, Persian King Darius with a 700,000-strong army and 600 ships made an unsuccessful attempt to conquer the Scythians, who had settled most of Ukraine. However, the Scythians were unrivaled equestrians and archers and kept evading a decisive battle with the Persians. While retreating to the east, they destroyed cropland and wells in their wake, raided caravans, and launched intermittent surprise attacks on the army of Darius from all sides. Darius was forced to return from this campaign with great losses.

Scythians made numerous attempts to conquer Greek colonies on the shores of the Black Sea. Their last known attempt to conquer then Roman cities in Crimea dates back to the first half of

In the late 2nd century BC, Chersonesus and Panticapaeum—with the help of Mithridates, ruler of the Kingdom of Pontus, repelled an attempt by Scythians to conquer them (Warning Bell in Chersonesus. Source: Wikipedia).

the 1st century BC. Roman troops successfully cleared the Scythian siege of Chersonesus (now Sevastopol), and it was the last historical mention of Scythians in Ukraine. They were, in turn, and after 2-3 centuries of warfare, dispossessed of their Ukrainian land by Sarmatian (Roxolani) tribes.

The Sarmatians, who like the Scythians – were very accomplished equestrians and warriors, were highly valued mercenaries and considered to be among the best in the imperial cavalry. Some of them even served on the British Isles. Perhaps this has something to do

It was only after the arrival of the Romans that a relative calm prevailed in the northern Black Sea colonies that effectively became part of the Roman Empire and received its protection from time to time (until the 4th century AD) against unruly neighbors: initially against Sarmatians-Roxolani and eventually Germanic tribes of Goths.

with Hollywood's production of the legend of King Arthur and his Sarmatian root.

The Germanic tribes of Goths arrived in the late 2nd to early 3rd centuries AD from northwestern Europe. For almost two centuries, after partly uniting the Sarmatians and Alans under their rule, they inhabited the lands of what are now Ukraine and Romania from where they launched successful campaigns against Roman provinces on the Balkan Peninsula and in Asia Minor (modern day Turkey).

What bears remembering is that the territory of Ukraine is not only the geographical center of Europe but also that the academic consensus identifies the Pontic-Caspian steppes (including Ukraine) as the "home" of almost all native European languages. If bloodlines and languages were the standard, Ukrainians can readily claim to be descendants of the multi-ethnic original Europeans.

It was not, however, until the passing of centuries and various other tribes and societies had come, settled, and moved on that Ukraine's evolution (as was Europe's) also started being shaped by forces that are now recognized as the third core component in the foundation of "European civilization"- Christianity.

At the end of the II century B.C., when the Greek cities of Chersonesus and Panticapae in the Crimea, with the help of the Pontic king Mithridates, repelled an attempt to conquer them by the Scythians, another Greek colony on the territory of Ukraine – Pontic Olbia (the region of modern Odessa) defended itself against the attack of the Celtic tribes – the Gauls. Let's remember this fact because one of the theories of the origin of the state of Rus – «Ruthenia» – has Gaulish roots [6].

According to this historical version, a part of the Gaulish tribe of the Ruthenians, after the conquest of Gaul (modern France) by Caesar, did not finally submit to the Romans. In the I century A.D., the part of the Ruthenians migrated across the Danube and Carinthia to the region of the Greek colony – the city of Hermonos. The colony was founded by the Greeks in the VI century B.C. on the Taman Peninsula, near the Crimea. According to Caesar's «Notes on the Gallic War», the Ruthenians were one of the most developed and freedom-loving tribes of the Gauls with whom he fought.

This was facilitated by their connections, over the centuries, with the Greek colonies on the shores of the Mediterranean Sea. For example, the Greek city of Messalia is the modern French city of Marseille. The Ruthenians, like the Greeks, were good sailors. Some of them knew the Greek language and knew the sea routes to the northern Black Sea colonies of the Greeks. They could have participated in or known about the attempted Celtic capture of Pontic Olbia at the end of the II century B.C., as well as about the nature and living conditions in the northern Black Sea and the Pryazovia region.

Having settled in the I century A.D. on the Taman Peninsula near the Greek city of Hermonos, the Ruthenians lived for several centuries next to the local Greeks, Tauri, Scythians, and later Goths.

Let us note that the historiographer of the French king Louis XIII – Jacques de Charron in the work «World history of all nations and especially the Gauls, or the French» in 1621 asserted that the Gauls – Ruthenians took part in the founding of the state of Ruthenia with its centre in Kyiv. For this, they rose, at one time, from the south to the north: across the Black Sea along the water artery of the Dnipro, to Kyiv. In this way, civilizational and cultural expansions in Europe took place prior to the 5th century A.D. They moved along the only highways of that time – sea and river arteries from the Mediterranean Sea, from south to north... [26]

The legend of the foundation in the V century A.D. of Kyiv, as the capital of the medieval state of the three brothers Kyi, Shchek and Khoryv and their sister Lybid, may have a new reading in this regard...

The first Christian priests to spread the Christian faith (in the form of Arianism) in the land of what is now Ukraine were Gothic priests. The Goths started adopting the Christian faith *en masse* from Christians in the provinces they captured, and especially so after the conquest of Crimea where Christianity first arrived back in the 1st century AD with Saint Clement. The spread of Christianity

Jacques de Charron Histoire universelle de toutes nations, et specialement des Gaulois ou François"

was greatly facilitated after the proclamation of religious tolerance throughout the Roman Empire in 313 AD and adoption of Christianity as the state religion in 380 AD. During the Gothic presence in Crimea in the 3rd-4th centuries AD, Chersonesus became one of the biggest centers for spreading Christianity throughout the northern Black Sea region.

Origins and spread of Christianity and borders of the Roman Empire in the 4th century.
Source: educational site on geography, world history, and history of Ukraine:
https://geomap.com.ua/uk-wh6/1145.html

Although the Goths can be credited with the rapid spread of Christianity, the other inhabitants of Ukraine first encountered that religion in the 1st century AD with the arrival of Saint Clement who was to become the 4th pope of Rome. He was sentenced by Emperor Trajan to penal servitude in local stone quarries in Crimea for spreading Christianity. When he arrived he already found converts among the local population and in the penal colony and established the first Christian parish in the territory of Ukraine.

750 years later, after his martyrdom, St. Clement's relics were taken to Rome from Crimea by two Bulgarian priests, Cyril and Methodius, who had devised the first alphabet to be used for Sla-

vonic manuscripts. Pope Adrian II received the relics and interred them in what is now the Basilica of Saint Clement. In 866 Pope Adrian added the Slavic language to Latin Greek and Hebrew as approved for divine service, and ordered that books translated into Slavic be placed in Roman Catholic churches.

Therefore, historical studies produce a convincingly affirmative answer to at least one question about Ukraine's European identity: it, alone, of all the post-Soviet republics, hosted, participated, influenced, and was influenced in the development of all three core elements of the historical foundation of European civilization.

Response to Putin's claim about the "sacral nature" of Crimea

In the context of what has been noted above regarding the spread of Christianity in the territory of Rus-Ukraine, we cannot help but rebut the hypothesis first proclaimed by Russian President Putin in 2014 and repeated by him on multiple occasions about the "sacral significance" of Crimea for Russia. Allegedly, it is where the "spiritual roots of modern Russia are concentrated" based on Prince Volodymyr's ("the Great") baptism in ancient Korsun (Chersonesus)".

Photo Reuters

This hypothesis is nothing new; it was first raised by Russian empress Catherine II who was obsessed with her so-called "Greek project" of gaining recognition for the Russian empire as the rightful (third) successor to the Holy Roman Empire after the capture of Byzantium by the Muslims.

Catherine II dreamed of seeing her second grandson Constantine ascends to the throne of Constantinople. Therefore (according to her twisted logic) the annexation of Crimea was not a land grab but merely the liberation of the Byzantine heritage from the Muslims, reclamation of primordial Greek Orthodox land, and – most importantly – restoration of Byzantium's legacy by way of Muscovy and the Russian empire. The religious rationale behind this hypothesis was that the baptism of Prince Volodymyr allegedly took place in Chersonesus, ergo the light of Christianity came to Rus from there, and in this way Rus accepted baptism from Byzantium in Chersonesus rather than from Kyiv.

Although Putin floated this myth to provide a religious justification for the annexation of Crimea, we know of no serious historian who would subscribe to a theory so bizarre as to warrant going to war and asserting a claim to another's land. Putin's "justification" (intended for domestic consumption) is based on a widely refuted religious event allegedly conducted over 1000 years ago and involving a ruler who was a stranger to, and had no historical relationship with, the claimant (Russia) at the time (988 AD) when Muscovy (Russia) did not even exist. Furthermore, Putin must be aware that the "claim" serves the dual purpose of asserting an entirely illusory "right of succession" to a fictional distinction that no one other than Russians seem to care about.

In other words, Putin's speech writers did a disservice to their president by opting for the propaganda-unfriendly topic of the true history in which Crimea is portrayed as a "sacral symbol" for modern-day Russia.

Let's turn to the opinion of an American historian and a highly respected intellectual on both continents, Prof. Timothy Snyder. He has observed that "the example of Crimea lays bare a problem within Putin's thinking. The idea that there is some sort of 'immutable civilization,' outside of time and human agency, always turns out to be based upon nothing. In the case of Crimea, Putin's notion that the peninsula was 'always' Russia is absurd, in almost more ways than one can count."

Notwithstanding the bizarre nature of Putin's claims and assertions, Prof. Snyder further demonstrates "the threadbare nature of his historical evidence: First of all, the historical event itself is not at all clear. One source says that Volodymyr was baptized in Crimea, as Putin likes to say; others that he was baptized in Kyiv. None of the sources date from the period itself, and so we cannot be certain that it took place at all, let alone of the locale. (If Volodymyr was indeed baptized in Crimea, Putin's logic would seem to suggest that the peninsula belongs to modern Greece, since the presumed site was part of Byzantium at the time)."

Prof Snyder continues by observing that Volodymyr was not a Russian. "There were no Russians at the time. He was the leader of a clan of Scandinavian warlords who had established a state in Kyiv, having wrenched the city from the control of Khazars. His clan was settling down, and the conversion to Christianity was part of the effort to build a state. It was called 'Rus,' apparently from a Finnish word for the slave trading company that brought the Vikings to Kyiv in the first place. It was not called 'Rus' because of anything to do with today's Russia — nor could it have been, since there was no Russia then, and no state would bear that name for another seven hundred years. Moscow, the city, did not exist at the time".

As Prof. Snyder correctly noted, Moscow was established more than a half century after Volodymyr's formal acceptance of Christianity as the Grand Prince of Kyiv in 988. Christianity, therefore, came to Muscovy from Kyiv and not from Chersonesus, and it required almost a century to suppress paganism in those northeastern regions of Kyiv's empire.

Second, even before Volodymyr's 10th century reign, St. Clement established the first Christian parish in Crimea in the 1st century and two centuries later the Goths were spreading Christianity in Crimea and Kyiv-Rus. Putin's claim that Volodymyr's alleged baptism in Crimea was the entry point for Christianity in Muscovy is entirely fictitious.

Snyder concluded that "Baptism, whatever its other merits, does not create some kind of timeless continuum of power over whatever range of territory some later figure chooses to designate. If it did, international relations would certainly look very different.

"This is the essence of colonial logic: only we, the colonizers, have a history; anyone whom we encounter along the way does not. For the purposes of a colonial war, this logic must be insisted upon, even if it rests on the wisp of a baptism.

To end where I began, though: in the basic legal sense, none of this matters. Legally speaking, Crimea is part of Ukraine for the same reason that Maine is part of the United States, or Provence is part of France: international law and the principle of mutual state

CRIMEAN ROULETTE
Claimed by Russia in 1783,
Crimea was made part of
Ukraine in 1954. With the
1991 collapse of the Soviet
Union, it remained in
Ukraine, but the Russian
Black Sea Fleet was allowed
to stay in Sevastopol.

Crimea is an autonomous region in Ukraine. The Crimean population has shown much stronger support for Russia than Ukrainians in Kiev and the West.
Map by Jerome Cookson, National Geographic
https://blog.education.nationalgeographic.org/2014/03/06/history-of-crimea-in-six-maps/

recognition. Even were Putin's arguments about Crimea and Ukraine something else than multidimensional nonsense, they would provide no justification for invasion and annexation" [25].

Byzantine Empire: a Path of Ideas in Space and Time

The Byzantine Empire was the first Christian empire in the history of mankind that existed longer than all known empires (330-1453 AD) and was instrumental in the spread of Christendom to one-fifth of the surface of the earth. The capital of the Byzantine Empire was Constantinople, which preserved the heritage of the ancient Greek and Roman cultures and civilizations for about a thousand years after the demise of the Western Roman Empire in

Byzantine Empire in its heyday. Source: educational site on geography, world history, and history of Ukraine: (https://geomap.com.ua/images/wh7a/Maps/02_2.jpg)

476 AD, and laid the groundwork for the Renaissance in Western Europe. It is precisely because of this continuity of Hellenic and Roman culture and civilization that Constantinople merited the title of the "Second Rome", and its empire as the "rightful successor to the Holy Roman Empire".

Constantine the Great (272–337 AD), the founder of the Byzantine Empire, was a Roman emperor. On May 11, 330, he announced the move of his empire's capital from Rome to the Greek city of Byzantium on the European bank of the Bosporus.

In those days the Roman Empire still stretched from the British Isles across the territories of modern-day France, Germany, Italy, and Spain all the way to northern Africa, the Balkan Peninsula, and what is now Turkey. Permanent Roman garrisons were stationed

The Roman Empire and locations where legions were stationed as of 125 AD. Source: Wikimedia Commons (https://upload.wikimedia.org/wikipedia/commons/b/bb/Roman_Empire_125.png)

in what is now Ukraine: in Olbia, Chersonesus, and Tyras along the north Black Sea coast.

The greatest achievement of this first Christian emperor was his proclamation of Christianity as the state religion. In doing so he not only kept the Roman Empire alive by giving it a chance to continue for another 1,000 years while impacting the civilization of the entire surrounding world.

As one proof of Ukraine's European identity, we have demonstrated previously that the territory of what is now Ukraine had been home to all three core elements of the ancient historical foundation of European civilization. If we look at these three as elements of the foundation, the walls built atop this foundation would be the products and ideas of the Renaissance in Italy and France; the Reformation in Germany, England, France, Switzerland, and other European countries; and the era of humanism – primarily in France with its Great French Revolution.

But would all of those momentous developments have been possible without the millennia-long chain that linked the foun-

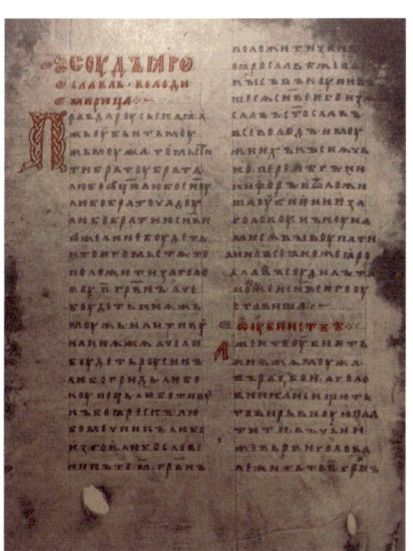 

First page of the Synodal List of Ruska Pravda: "COURT OF YAROSLAV VOLODYMYROVYCH. RUSKA PRAVDA..." and the golden chest where Ruska Pravda is stored.
Source: https://www.wikiwand.com/uk/Руська_Правда.

dation of this civilization beginning in the 5th century BC with its products and ideas that began appearing in Europe, for example in the 15th century during the Renaissance? Would the Napoleonic Civil Code have been possible without the existence of the Byzantine *Code of Justinian* before it? And would it have had such an impact on the continued evolution of the modern European system of law without the groundwork laid by Britain's *Magna Carta Libertatum*, *Ruska Pravda* of Yaroslav the Wise, and Germany's *Magdeburg Law*, all of which had been created on the basis of the *Code of Justinian*?

These questions are rather rhetorical because they had already been answered throughout history. The Byzantine Empire was the first to start the mass practice of transferring the precious knowledge of previous human civilizations from papyrus scrolls into manuscripts that soon flooded Europe. They inspired both the Renaissance process in Europe and the great geographical discoveries in the New World.

Without the Byzantine heritage, it would be hard to imagine the external and internal decor of St. Mark's Basilica in Venice; the most precious Christian relics in the Holy Chapel (Sainte-Chapelle) in Paris; as well as the *Reims Gospel* which Princess Anne, daughter of Yaroslaw the Wise of Kyiv, brought as a gift to her husband – Henry I, the King of France.

Eviscerated and pillaged for the first time by "Christian brethren" during the Fourth Crusade in 1204, Constantinople through its cultural and material treasures impacted the development of what would become Western Europe's most influential medieval kingdoms.

Most importantly for Ukrainians, the influence of Christianity and the culture of the Byzantine Empire played an exceedingly important role in the 10th-12th centuries AD in advancing one of the most powerful and advanced European states of that time – Kyivan Rus, the cradle of modern-day Ukraine. Meanwhile, it is hard to overestimate the impact that this Slavic state built with the active involvement of north European nations (Vikings-Varangians) had on the evolution of Europe. The court of Kyiv's Grand Prince became a hub for spreading Christianity and European culture to vast north-eastern European expanses. And Kyivan Rus ranked among the leading progressive states of Europe.

One of Kyiv's adjunct principalities that of Vladimir-Suzdal, which was founded in 1147 and later renamed Muscovy, was the largest beneficiary of Kyiv's Christianizing and civilizing influence. But that did not spare Kyiv from the destruction of 1169 when Prince Andrey Dolgorukiy of Vladimir Suzdal led a coalition that looted and plundered Kyiv for 3 days, and from which the city was never able to fully recover and avert the disastrous Mongol invasion of 1240. Andrey Dologrukiy is now recognized by historians as the first "Russian" ruler because of the alienation of his realm from that of Kyivan-Rus....an alienation that persists to this day.

Kyivan Rus from an Unexpected Angle. Sviatoslav the Brave, Bulgaria, Karl Marx, and Ukrainian self-identification

The latest discoveries in academic and applied genetic studies, combined with a more thorough reinterpretation of known historical sources, have opened new opportunities for a more complete assessment of Rus-Ukraine, including its links with ancient Bulgaria, as well as the validity of labeling Ukrainians "Lesser Russians".

We begin with the unfinished book by Karl Marx, *Secret Diplomatic History of the Eighteenth Century*, in which he studies the history of the origin of Muscovy and Russia and analyzes the foreign policy of czarist governments prior to 1860 [14]. Although Marx's social policies and political theories proved ruinous to millions of people, he was considered a competent historian of his time. It is interesting that despite his idolization by the Soviet state, this book had never been published in the Russian empire and first appeared in the USSR only a few years before its collapse. Consider what he writes:

"As the empire of Charlemagne precedes the foundation of modern France, Germany, and Italy, so the empire of the Rurikids (*Rus with its capital in Kyiv – Auth.*) precedes the foundation of Poland, Lithuania, the Baltic Settlements, Turkey, and Muscovy itself... The history of Muscovy is threaded to the history of Rus... The bloody mire of Mongolian slavery, not the rude glory of the Norman epoch, forms the cradle of Muscovy, and modern Russia is but a metamorphosis of Muscovy... Even after its liberation (*from the Mongol yoke in the 15th century – Auth.*) Muscovy continued to play its traditional role of a slave turned master".

Here is an interesting question: Why was this particular book hushed up and banned for more than a century in the Russian empire and later in the USSR even though it had been authored by

Karl Marx – a classic and founder of the "Marxist-Leninist science and ideology" that was dogma in the USSR?

Karl Marx believed that ancient Rus with its capital in Kyiv was not a mono-Slavic state, but a Gothic empire of the Rurikids (9th-11th centuries), which had the same historical and civilizing influence on the development of eastern europe as the Frankish empire of Charlemagne (8th-9th centuries AD) had on western Europe.

Notably, the word "empire" has key significance here. The ancient Celtic countries of Gaul and Britain were part of the Roman Empire, but their descendants, the French and the British, did not call themselves Romans, and did not appropriate the entirety of Roman history and its Etruscan beginnings to themselves.

The Frankish emperor Charlemagne is celebrated as a national hero and founder of two powerful states – Germany and France. And yet Napoleon Bonaparte did not attempt to use this as an excuse to rewrite the history of French and German lands, and brand the Bavarians, Swabians, or Saxons (who were previously part of the empire of Germanic Franks) as "the Lesser French".

Likewise, the natives of Novgorod, Vladimir-Suzdal, and eventually Muscovy were part and parcel of the Rurikids Empire and subordinated as vassals to the Grand Court of Kyivan Rus. Yet this did not automatically entitle them to start calling themselves "Greater Russians" in the 18th century and brand the direct descendants and founders of the empire as "Lesser Russians" [22]….or any kind of "Russians" for that matter.

There was something even more threatening to the official historiography of Russia than the fact that Karl Marx emphasized what he believed to be Russia's identity theft and hijacking of the historical heritage of ancient Rus, or even his insistence on the Norman-Scandinavian origins of its statehood. The biggest threat to Russia and Soviet authorities was Marx's reasoned conclusions and identification of the very nature of the Rurikids dominion as being "Gothic" and not Slavic!

This directly challenged not only the official history of the new empire written after Peter (the 1st), but also all of its foreign policy that had historically (since the time of Catherine II) revolved around the proclamation of Russia's exclusive rights to protection of pan-Slavism and Orthodoxy on a global scale. Even Soviet historical science attempted to overlook the Gothic issue for a long time because it undermined the underlying concept according to which Russia, Ukraine, and Belarus are "one nation" and the collective "cradle" of east European Slavism. That is why, according to Soviet historians, there could not have existed any distinctly divergent state formations in the land prior the formation of a collective unitary state by three "brotherly" peoples. Moreover, there could not have been a Gothic state because the Goths are ancestors of contemporary Germans, and the Gothic issue was of great interest to the Nazis.

Russian archaeologist Oleg Sharov writes: "The Goths are currently associated with the Wielbark culture discovered in Poland and the Santana de Mures—Chernyakhov culture discovered in the vast expanses of Ukraine, Russia, Moldova, and Romania. This was not always the case. For a long time, up until the late 1980s, the Chernyakhov culture was considered to be Slavic per the official opinion of Soviet science... The 'Gothic issue'— known in central Europe and Scandinavia as the search for the proto-homeland of the Goths and their migratory routes—acquired a political coloring in the postwar Soviet archaeological science. The "Slavism" of the cultures of the first centuries AD (Zarubintsy, Chernyakhov, Przeworsk cultures, etc.) was to be accepted as official dogma, and any ideas about the 'Germanic' nature of these cultures were tantamount to political sabotage..." [21].

Canadian historian O. Kovalevskyi has noted that soon after the Soviet Union was formed, the study of the history of the Goths was banned, and their presence in the territory of what is now Ukraine was either denied or concealed. It was only in the 1960s that the following admission was made in response to new archaeological and historical sources: Indeed, the Goths were present, but only in Crimea and only within the thin strip of its southern coast [11].

Kyiv (Slavic) and Chernyakhov (Gothic) cultures. Migratory routes of the Goths in the 2ⁿᵈ-3ʳᵈ centuries. Source: Wikipedia: https://www.wikiwand.com/ru//Черняховская_культура

Ukrainian historian Yevhen Synytsia writes that "although for contemporary archaeologists and historians the notable role of the Goths in creating the colorful Chernyakhov artifacts is not open to any serious debate, the public at large still lives in the past. This is no surprise because the Chernyakhov culture is treated as Slavic or at least predominantly Slavic in school textbooks and largely even in university course books)" [16].

What we also know to be a historical fact is that prior to the founding of the Kyivan-Rus state, the territory that is now known as Ukraine was named Scythia and Sarmatia in the later half of the 1st nillenia BC and early centuries AD and later much of it was known as Gothia. These designations were never applied to any part of the territories to the north of Ukraine in what we now know as "Russia".

As the most recent and dominant residents of large areas of Ukraine prior to the Kyivan- Rus state, and, therefore, the ones who are most likely to have had the largest influence on contemporary

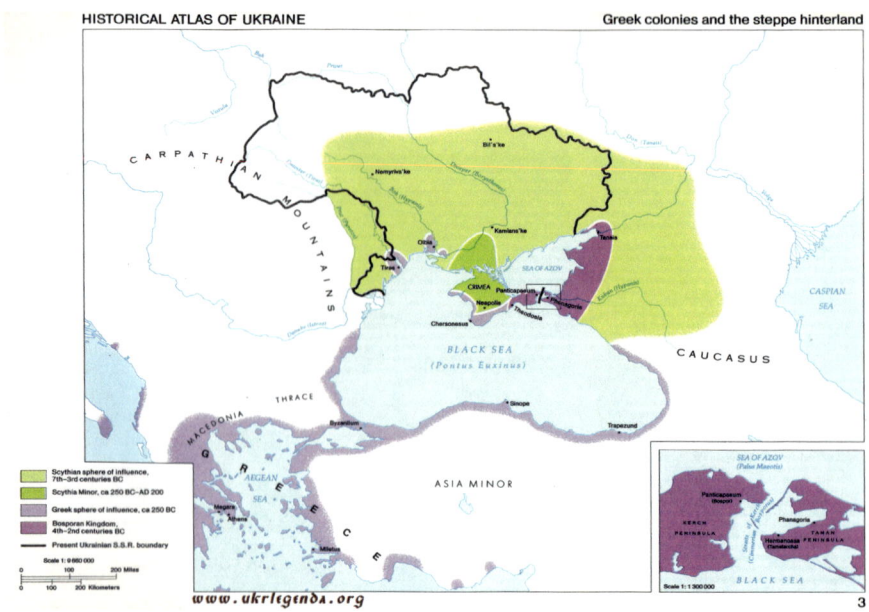

Scythian sphere of influence (7th–3rd centuries BC), Lesser Scythia (approx. 250 BC — 200 AD) and the Greek sphere of influence (approx. 250 BC). Illustration from Paul Robert Magocsi's book "History of Ukraine", Toronto, 1996 (https://history.ed-era.com/mizh_russyu_ta_richchyu_knyazyvstvo_feodoro)

Ukrainians, the Goths merit special attention from historians and archaeologists. The Goths arrived in Ukraine in the late 2nd – early 3rd centuries AD through what is now Poland and most likely coming from southern Scandinavia (modern-day southern Sweden and the Swedish island of Gotland). From 1278 to 1973, the title of the king of Sweden included the words: "We, …, by the Grace of God, King of the Swedes, Goths…", while the colors of the national flags of Sweden and Ukraine are both yellow and blue.

For about two centuries (3th – 5th centuries AD), after partly uniting the remaining Scythians, Sarmatians, and Alans under their rule, the Goths lived mostly in Ukraine, Moldova, and Romania and formed one of the first Gothic state formations in Ukraine.

Towards the end of this state's existence, its imperial western borders reached as far as Bulgaria, while its eastern borders extended to the Ural Mountains [1].

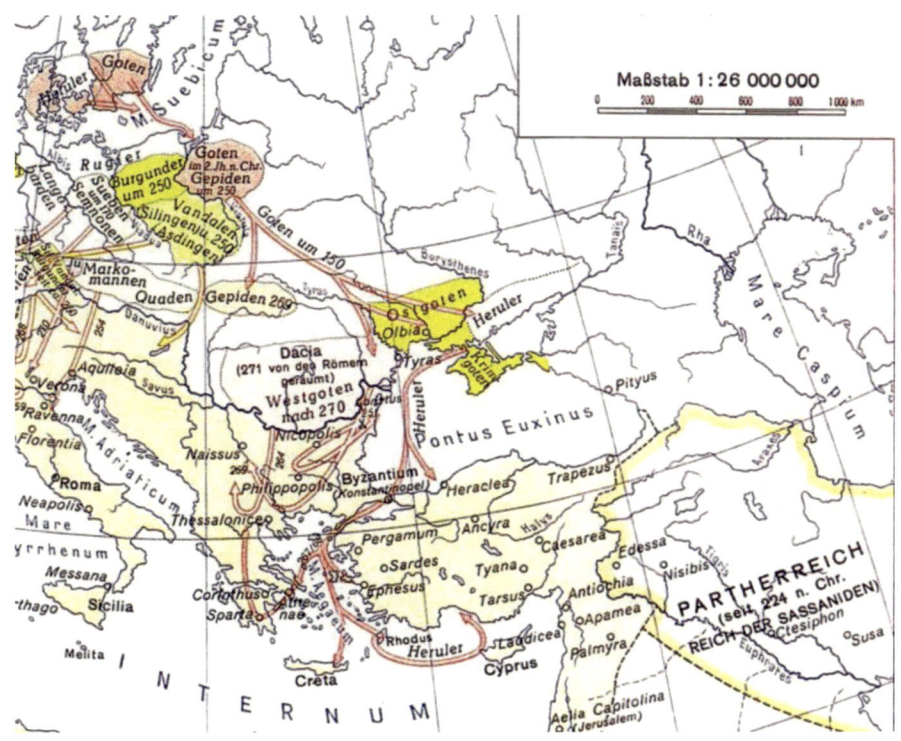

A German map showing the migration of Goths to and across Ukraine in the 2nd and 3rd centuries AD. Paul Robert Magocsi, "History of Ukraine", Toronto, 1996 (http://www.conflicts.rem33.com/images/Ukraine/Early%20History.htm)

During this time, the Goths launched successful raids into provinces of the Roman Empire on the Balkan Peninsula and in Asia Minor (modern-day Turkey). They left particularly tangible traces in Crimea where they preserved their own Gothic language until the 16th century. It wasn't until the 18th century that the Crimean Goths began to vanish from the local population [9, 6].

The Crimean Goths adopted Christianity in the late 3rd century. The Gothic alphabet (27 characters based on Greek and Latin letters) was invented by the Gothic Christian Bishop Ulfilas as early as the 4th century in order to translate the Holy Bible. The Gothic Bible is the first literary work in one of the Germanic languages.

The Gothic state reached its heyday under King Ermanaric. Illustration from the publication titled "Apocalypse 375. Collapse of the First Civilizational Project of Eastern Europe". Dilettante journal, February 2012 (http://elteber.narod.ru/index/0–24)

Disaster struck the Goths in 375 AD when the Huns invaded from the east. Unable to ward off the Huns for long, the most militant faction together with the chiefs were forced to gradually retreat westward from their settlements in Ukraine. These "Eastern Goths" (commonly known as "Ostrogoths") – erstwhile compatriots of the residents they left behind in Ukraine – moved on to conquests in the Balkans and an invasion into Italy. Together with another Germanic tribe, the Langobards, they mixed and married with the native Italians. The Goths who remained in Ukraine continued to mix with old and new tribes and ethnic groups until fully assimilating with the native population.

The Ostrogoths played an active part in the liberation of Europe from the Huns and in the final destruction of the Western Roman Empire. They conquered Rome, absorbed some of the Roman

The Hunnic Empire in 450 AD.

East-Slavic tribes in the 8th – 9th centuries. Source: Wikimedia Commons (https://commons.wikimedia.org/wiki/File:East_Slavic_tribes_peoples_8th_9th_century.jpg)

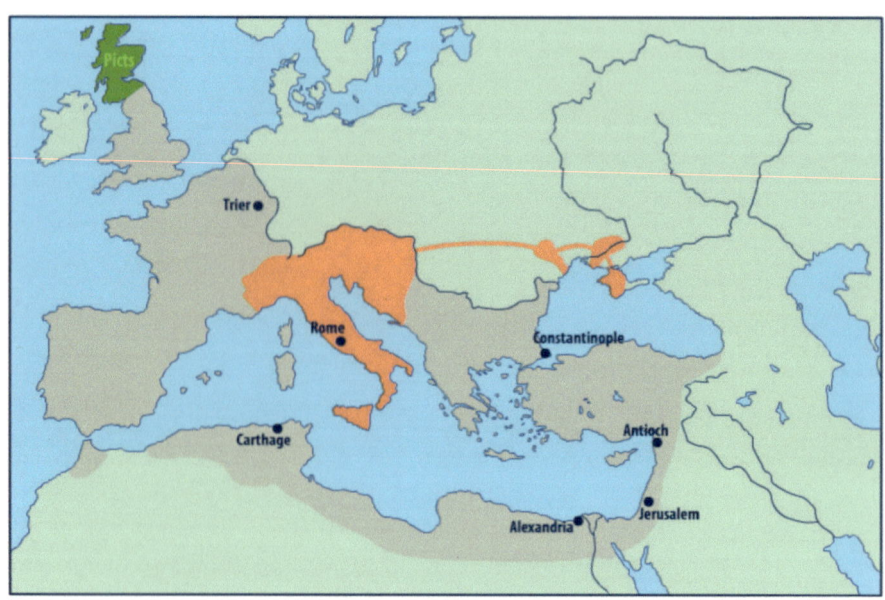

The illustration depicts the migration of the Ostrogoths into Western Europe (article "The Great Migration of Peoples into the Western Roman Empire... Barbarian Raids Beginning in 395 AD" (https://www.animatedmaps.div.ed.ac.uk/Divinity6web/movements.html)

culture, and founded the first feudal kingdoms of the early middle Ages in Western Europe: in Italy, Spain, Southern France, and Austria. Ostrogoth King Theodoric (475-526) is considered to be the founder of the Italian Kingdom.

Over time their name, much like the names of other tribes and nations of that time, sank into oblivion in Western Europe as they assimilated with, and settled into, the new nations they conquered. The northwestern, mountainous part of the Crimean Peninsula between Sudak and Balaklava had been called Gothia almost until the mid-19th century [5]. The Crimean Goths also had their own Principality of Theodoro in the middle Ages until they were forced in 1778 to resettle to the shores of the Sea of Azov under pressure from the Turks. Here, led by the last Gothic Metropolitan Archbishop Ignatius, they founded the city of Mariupol and 24 villages that are part of Ukraine.

The second wave of colonization of Ukrainian land – this time by the Varangians –Normans ensued during the period of Byzantium's preeminence in Europe. It was then that the empire of the Rurikids with its center in Kyiv came into being and expanded rapidly in the aftermath of numerous military campaigns waged by Sviatoslav Ihorovych (935-972 AD), the Grand Prince of Kyiv and the last non-Christian ruler of Rus. Sviatoslav ("the Conqueror") was the grandson of the Varangian Rurik, legendary founder of Rus, and the son of Princess Olga, the daughter of Vladimir of Bulgaria.

In addition to conquering the tribes of the Radimichs and Vyatichs (whose territories later became the empire's principalities of Chernihiv, Rostov-Suzdal, and Ryazan) as well as Volga Bulgarians and Alans, he also caused the final decline of the Khazar "Khanate" and the First Bulgarian Empire. His first Bulgarian campaign resulted in the conquest of Bulgaria and eventually in one more cam-

Kingdoms of Western and Eastern Goths and the Eastern Roman Empire in 526 AD: map from the archives of EmersonKent.com
(http://www.emersonkent.com/map_archive/germanic_roman_526.htm)

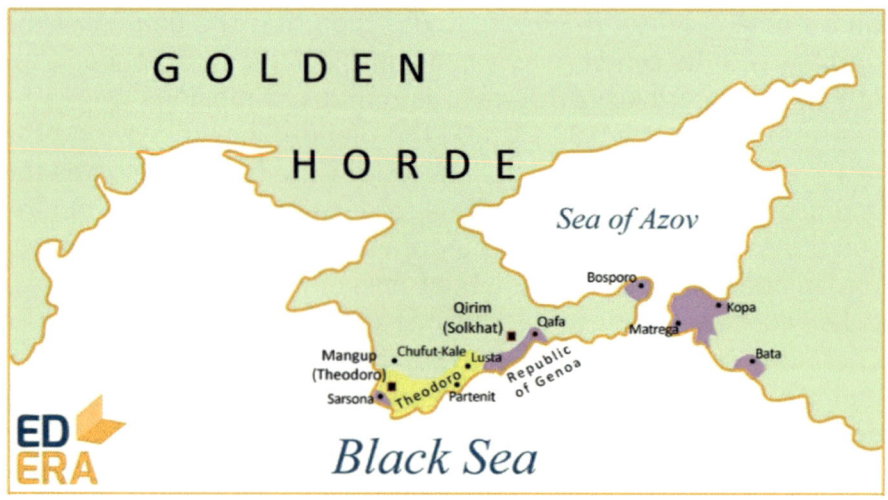

Principality of Theodoro. Illustration from "The History of Ukraine" – a joint project of the Ministry of Education and the EdEra online education studio (https://edera.gitbook.io/ed-era-book-history/mizh_russyu_ta_richchyu/ knyazyvstvo_feodoro)

paign (together with the Bulgarians) against Constantinople. After several victories over the Byzantines, this campaign ended in Svia- toslav's defeat by Byzantine emperor John I Tzimiskes in the Battle of Silistra, and a forced peace treaty with the Byzantine Empire. Sviatoslav met a treacherous death in a Pecheneg ambush on the Dnipro rapids upon his return to Kyiv in 972.

In the aftermath of the two Bulgarian campaigns undertaken by Sviatoslav, Rus and Byzantium established a special (*strategic*, in modern parlance) relationship. Rus no longer attempted direct campaigns against Constantinople, the capital of the Byzantine em- pire, or its adjacent lands, but limited itself to an infrequent show of force against the empire's Crimean lands. In addition, its emper- ors were personally secured by an elite Varangian mercenary guard and could occasionally rely on military assistance from Rus. In exchange, Rus formally received Christianity from Byzantium, and, thereby, was accepted by Christian Europe's potentates and induct- ed fully into its Greece-Roman civilization.....as well as preferential trading terms along the famous Varangian to Greek trade route.

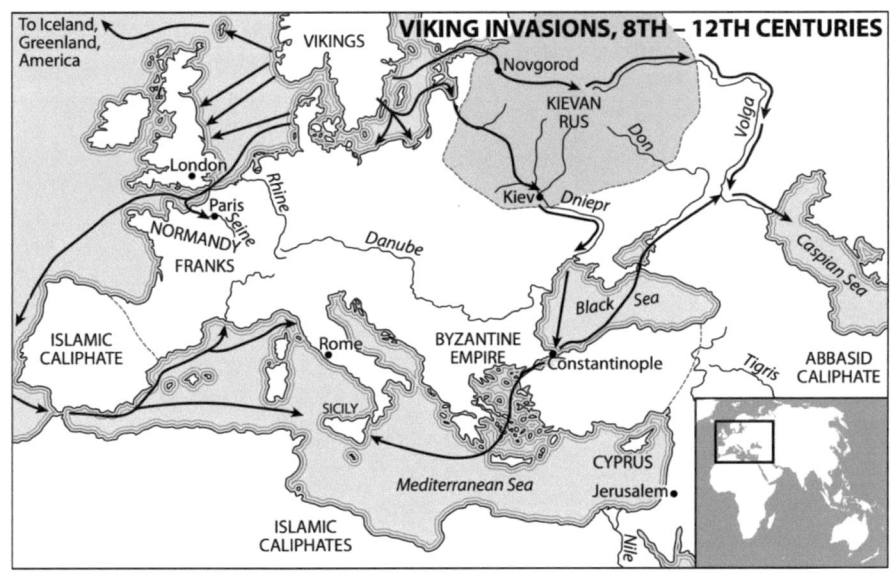

Viking invasion routes—Illustration from "The Brief History of the World" published on the GoodReads.com website owned by Amazon.com (https://media.bloomsbury.com/rep/files/2.2a%20-%20Viking%20Invasions,%208th%20to%2012%20Centuries%20%5BSH%5D.jpg)

In the essay titled "European Civilization... and Ukraine" above, we demonstrated that Christianity first arrived in the territory of what is now Ukraine back in the 1st century AD with Saint Clement, But the mass spread of Christianity in the south of modern-day Ukraine began under the Germanic Goths in the 3rd – 5th centuries AD. Ancient Chersonesus (Korsun) was the hub through which Christianity spread in the northern Black Sea region.

In the 10th century, Kyiv became the center for the spread of Christianity and Byzantine culture to the northeastern lands of its empire, and not the other way around. This means that the Christian church of Kyiv is much older than that of Moscow. According to written sources, after Volodymyr the Great baptized Kyivans in 988, the natives of Novgorod had to be baptized with the help of "the cross of voivode Dobrynya (Volodymyr's uncle) and the sword of voivode Putyata". As late as 1024, volkhv (heathen shamans) in the land of Suzdal staged a rebellion against the Christian faith and

Rus-Byzantine Treaty of 971 (Radziwill Chronicle, sheet 88). Source: Wikimedia Commons (https://commons.wikimedia.org/wiki/File:Русско-византийский_договор_971_года.jpg?uselang=uk)

church. Moscow had not even existed at the time.

Yet even the founder of Moscow – Grand Prince of Kyiv Yuri Dolgorukiy, who descended not only from Byzantine emperors but also from the last Anglo-Saxon King Harold – would probably never predict that his son (Prince Andrey of Vladimir-Suzdal) would so treacherously and cruelly "return the kindness" of Kyiv, "the mother of Rus cities".

In 1169, Andrey along with other northern Rus princes pillaged and destroyed the capital of the empire of the Rurikids – ancient Kyiv. Without Kyiv, the cities of Vladimir, Suzdal and Moscow would not have been established. This represented the final breakup between these former vassal princedoms and the cultural heritage of the "Gothic empire of the Rurikids". By destroying Kyiv, Andrey objectively laid the groundwork for the final destruction and collapse of Kyivan Rus by the Mongols in 1240. In 1223, the grand princes of Suzdal and their vassals did not even join the first battle of Rus against the Mongol Tatars on the River Kalka. Their Moscow descendants became skilful administrators of Mongol tributes and grateful imitators of their despotic rule.

Crown or Stigma?

Historians have long since separated these intrinsically and semantically different words: "Ruthenian" and "Russian", "Rus / Ruthenia" and "Russia". Yet because history has been used as a tool of political struggle, even the majority of European languages do not have different terms for these historically different words. The fact is that it was not until the 18th century that direct descendants of the "Rus people" – Ukrainians, who formed the core of the medieval empire of Rus and had previously been called "Ruthenians" were renamed "Lesser Russians" in the Russian empire. This gave the numerically superior Finno-Ugric and Turkic ethnic groups from the "Vladimir-Suzdal lands" (formerly vassals of Kyiv) a rationale for calling themselves "Greater Russians".

But when exactly did the Rurikids Empire and its former vassal province of Vladimir Suzdal part ways and the latter began creating an Asian model of despotism in the new Muscovy? The answer lies in the course of that empire's four centuries of growth and rule.

History indicates that the cultural, religious, and educational influence of Rus-Ukraine both within its empire and on European evolution and development between the 8th and 13th centuries is hard to overestimate. This process took root and was greatly enhanced when two new waves of colonization came together in the land of what is now Ukraine. The first wave, which brought trade, infrastructure, and state-building, came from northern Europe (along the Varangian to Greek trade route). The second wave, which brought religion, culture, and education—came from southern Europe, from the Byzantine Empire. It was during this very time, from the 8th to the 12th centuries, that the second wave of Scandinavian colonization of Ukrainian lands (by the Varangians-Normans) was timed to coincide with the Byzantine Empire's cultural and civilizational domination. That is how the Ukrainian proto-state came into being: i.e., Rus – the empire of the Rurikids with its Kyiv metropolis

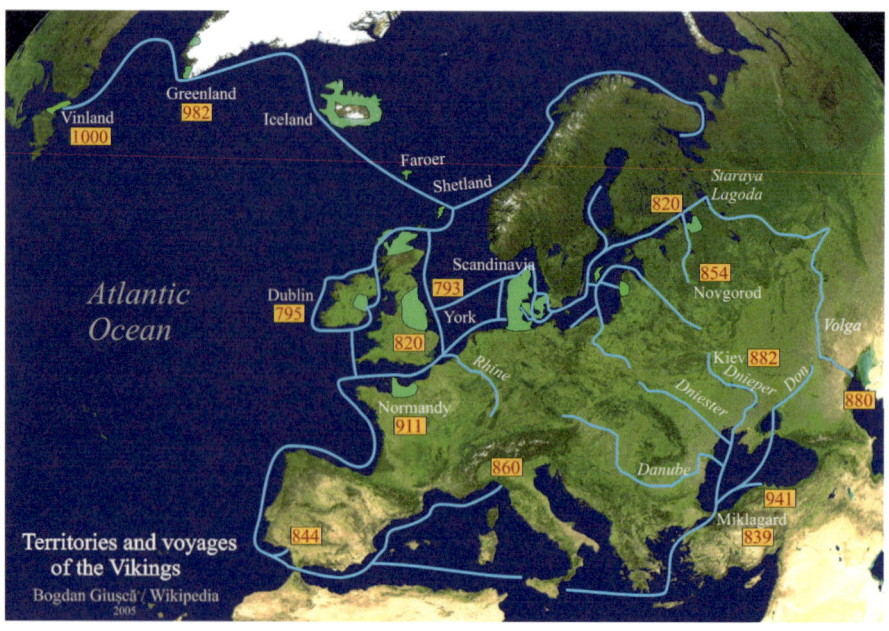

Viking territories and campaigns. Source: https://en.wikipedia.org/wiki/Viking_Age.

[6, 24]. But how did the Rurikids establish and govern the empire in distant Ukraine?

"The patronymic of the name 'Rurik' has Scandinavian roots. It is 'Hrod Ric', meaning 'Mighty in Glory'. After Vikings plundered several Frankish cities in the late 9th century, Frankish Emperor Lothair (grandson of Charlemagne) agreed to hand over the lands of the Frisians (now part of the Netherlands and Germany) to a Viking leader named Roric.

Shortly afterwards Roric may have gone in search of richer lands before allegedly reappearing on the ice-covered River Volkhov.

It is in this context that the monk, Nestor, mentions the Kyivan "Polany" tribe in 862. The Polany are looking for «a ruler who would rule and communicate with them according to the law....Our land is great..." they told the Varangians, "...and has everything except for law and order. Come, take it, and rule us...." [24]

And so the legendary Rurikids came to Kyiv through the lands of Pskov and Novgorod. Soon the Grand Princely Court of their state in Kyiv became the hub for spreading Christianity and the Byzantine form of European culture throughout the vast east European and partly Asian territories. The empire itself, Rus became a flagship of cultural progress in the common European history of the time for more than two centuries [6, 14, 24].

The names of the great princes and princesses of Kyiv – Oleh (Helge), Ihor (Ingvar), Olha (Helga), Sviatoslav (Sviataslaff), Volodymyr (Voldemar) the Great, Yaroslav (Yarislaff) the Wise, and Volodymyr (Voldemar) Monomakh are etched in historical chronicles where they are honored as monarchs who shaped European history.

Iconic mosaic images of the first ancient Rus saints, Volodymyr and Olha, are on display at St. Peter's Cathedral in Rome. These monarchs shared bloodlines with the emperors of Byzantium and the Holy Roman Emperor, the royal courts of Sweden, Norway, Denmark, France, England, Scotland, Poland, Hungary, Bohemia, and a series of German princedoms. The blood of their descendants coursed through the veins of the rulers of these states for centuries. Such venerated Christian saints as Saint Louis in France and Saint Margarita in Scotland are bloodline descendants of the Rurikids Grand Princes of Kyiv.

"The bloodline of Anne of Kyiv – the wife of French King Henry I and mother of Philip can be traced to all the monarchs of Europe from Philip of Edinburgh to Philippe I of Belgium, through Felipe VI of Spain, all of whom were named after her first son..." [24]. After Philip I of France, it became one of the most common names there. (*Note from author: Although the name of Apostle Philip who preached Christianity in Scythian lands was well known, it was not until the arrival of Anne of Kyiv in France that "Philip" became one of the most common royal names of western Europe*).

Before Anne became the Queen of France, her father -Yaroslav the Wise – ruled Europe's biggest country with some three to four million subjects. At the time, the lands of Yaroslav the Wise extended in the north to the territory of what is now Estonia. There he

Princedoms of Kyivan Rus (1054-1132). Source: Wikimedia Commons
*https://commons.wikimedia.org/wiki/Atlas_of_Ukraine#/media/File:Principalities_*
of_Kievan_Rus'_(1054-1132).jpg

founded a new city, Yuriyiv -"the city of Saint Yuri (George)". Yaroslav was given the name of this saint upon his baptism. Today this Estonian city is named Tartu. In the south and east, the lands of Yaroslav stretched all the way to the Caucasus Mountains.

Yet one of the biggest civilizational contributions to the spread of European culture, statehood, and Christianity came through a northeastern vassal principality of the empire of the Rurikids – the Rostov-Suzdal principality. Inhabited primarily by Finno-Ugric tribes this principality was eventually renamed Vladimir-Suzdal and was the birthplace for a new Eurasian state – Muscovy – in the 16th century (renamed "Russia" in the 18th century).

However, despite the empire's contributions, influence and notable success, it was not shared the scourge of intra-dynastic rivalries and even fratricide with tragic consequences for its own statehood. Andrey Bogolyubsky – vassal prince of Vladimir-Suzdal, son of the Grand Prince of Kyiv Yuri Dolgorukiy – failed to recognize that without Kyiv's civilizational role it may never have given rise to cities like Rostov (862 AD) or Suzdal (1024 AD). Nor would there have been a Moscow (first mentioned in 1047) as a separate appendage of the Vladimir-Suzdal principality.

Prince Andrei Bogolyubsky began his plundering and ruination of Rus, the capital of the empire, in 1155. That year he stole the icon of the Virgin Mary from a convent in Vyshhorod outside Kyiv and ran away with it to Vladimir-on-Klyazma. According to legend, this icon was painted by Saint Luke the Evangelist (during the Virgin Mary's lifetime in the 1st century AD), and brought to Kyiv from Constantinople in 1131. It immediately became the most venerated icon in Rus, and came to be known as the miracle-working icon of "Our Lady of Vladimir". To this day this stolen property is recognized as the greatest "Muscovite" icon and eventually the greatest "Russian icon".

To help you understand what it meant for medieval monarchs to possess Christian icons or relics, it is worth mentioning the example of the emissaries of Frankish King Henry I to Kyiv in 1048-1049. According to French chronicles, Bishop Roger of Chalon (leader of this delegation), at the request of the archbishop and prior of Reims Cathedral, consulted with Yaroslav the Wise regarding the fate of the relics of Saint Clement. The "King of Rus" responded by allowing the bishop to inspect the relics of St. Clements which were stored and venerated in the Church of the Tithes in Kyiv.

But Prince Andrey did not stop at stealing the icon of the Virgin Mary. Five years later he made his first failed attempt to establish a new metropolis of the empire in his own land. Nine years later, in 1169 the "son of the land of Suzdal" led an allied army of 11 northern princes together with nomadic Cuman tribes to lay siege to Kyiv. After a long seige, Kyiv was subjected to unprecedented devastation.

According to chronicles, natives of "Suzdal", "Smolensk", and "the Cumans" spent several days ransacking and burning "the mother of Rus cities". Large numbers of Kyivans had been taken captive and enslaved. Residential quarters and a large number of churches and monasteries were destroyed or burned to the ground. Not only treasures but also icons, bells, and vestments were stolen and removed from more than 400 monasteries and churches in Kyiv. The main metropolitan cathedral of the church of Rus – St. Sophia Cathedral, which stored the famous library of Yaroslav the Wise, was also looted barbarically for the first time.

Russian historians try not to mention the pogrom of Kyiv by Bogolyubsky, claiming that Kyiv had been destroyed by the Mongol Tatars. Chronicles prove, however, that "natives of Suzdal destroyed Kyiv to a point where the Mongol Tatars had no longer anything to destroy in 1240" [23]. After capturing Kyiv, Andrey gave the city over for three days of looting and plundering to his soldiers. It was accepted to treat cities this way only when dealing with foreign settlements. As pointed out by Lev Gumilyov, for Andrey and his army Kyiv was just as foreign as any German or Polish castle; in other words, the people of what is now Russia demonstrated no sense of ethnic and state unity with Kyivan Rus [4].

Andrey's Turkic nomadic ancestry (on his mother's side) may have alienated him from embracing his father's European heritage.

He was the first to "upend the political system of the Rus land" [10]. At first, in his own principality he did everything in his power to establish an unlimited authoritarian rule that bore greater resemblance to oriental despotism than European models of governance. He not only banished his stepmother (a Byzantine princess), his brothers, nephews, and the old clan nobility of his father from his land, but also banned *veche* (popular assemblies of citizens) in old *veche* cities (e.g.,Rostov and Suzdal) – a prototype of the culture of European self-governance that took the shape of the Magdeburg Law in Europe soon afterwards.

The destruction of the Rus empire's core economic and political power combined with severance from European state-building, and its cultural and civilizational traditions proved fatal for Rus. Kyiv lost its significance as a political, cultural, and economic center of the empire, which contributed to its subsequent conquest by the Mongol Tatars in 1240. [3, 10].

The fact of the matter is that international trade was the lifeblood of Kyiv's economy. It was based on the strategic placement of the empire's capital at a crossroads of two major trade routes: from the north of Europe to the south ("from the Varangians to the Greeks") and from the East to West ("Silk Road"). This was further bolstered by Kyiv's time-honored diplomatic and familial ties with both European and Byzantine monarchic dynasties.

The level of Christian and European cultural development of Kyiv at the time was also beyond comparison with those of Vladimir-on-Klyazma or Suzdal, let alone Moscow. Finally, the move of the capital city caused it to be farther removed geographically from Western Europe, the Black Sea, and the Baltic Sea, while bringing it closer to Asia. Given the medieval limitations of transportation and roads, this hampered the continued development of cultural, economic, and state-building ties with Europe.

Domestic strife among princes of the clan of the Rurikids (much like in other monarchic dynasties of Europe at the time) is not a historically unprecedented phenomenon – it had been known to happen before. However, these rivalries rarely destroyed the legal system that was in place or emerging at the time. Andrey's actions not only blocked Yaroslav's "Ruska Pravda", but even failed to introduce a replacement until 500 years later in the form of *Sobornoe Ulozhenie* ("Council Code") by Czar Aleksey Mikhaylovich Romanov. Meanwhile, the territory of what would become Muscovy was sidelined from trading routes for several centuries.

As for Western Europe, several centuries before these events there were other examples of dynastic disputes but without the fatal consequences, savagery, and destruction. In the 6th century, Clovis – the first Frankish king from the Merovingian dynasty also divided the empire up among his sons. Each one of them had a kingdom and a capital city of their own. However, the dynasty members decided that the shared capital of their empire, Paris, would remain the "sacred city" for the entire dynasty. None of the heirs was allowed to enter Paris on their own, without being accompanied by the other brothers, to say nothing of conquering or looting it.

"Prior to (*the destruction of Kyiv in 1169 – Auth.*), the rank of the senior grand prince was inextricably linked with possession of the Kyiv seat. True to custom, the prince who was recognized to be the most senior among relatives had his seat in Kyiv. Andrey was the first to separate seniority from the seat and do so by force. After forcing people to recognize him as the Grand Prince of the entire Rus land, he did not leave his Suzdal *volost* and did not go to Kyiv to take the seat held by his father and grandfather. So by separating themselves from the seat, senior princes no longer accorded the Kyiv metropolis the special deference it had enjoyed for several generations [10].

This destructive, east-oriented, and essentially Asian state-building policy of Prince Andrey Bogolyubsky was counterbalanced by a different west-oriented and European state-building policy pursued by Prince Roman Mstyslavovych. His father Mstyslav Izyaslavych – also a Rurikids – was the Grand Prince of Kyiv in 1167. He died in 1170 shortly after the pogrom of Kyiv by Andrey Bogolyubsky.

After these events his son, Prince Roman, united the lands of Volhynia and Galicia in the west to form the Principality of Galicia–

Volhynia. By 1200 AD he already controlled much of the lands in what is now right-bank Ukraine and proposed his own project to preserve unity and continue building the empire with its capital in Kyiv, to wit: "Brothers, you know that Kyiv is home to the highest throne in the land of Rus and it should be filled by the smartest and most senior of the brothers so that he would rule well and defend the land of Rus everywhere and maintain order among the brothers to keep them from slighting one another or attacking one another's land. Yet today we see the opposite being done: younger and incapable brothers launch attacks despite being unable to hold on to the land and bring order among the brothers, let alone defend themselves. This causes wars among brothers, who fetch the infidels who run the land of Rus and take away land from the brothers, which they covet very much...

"I will tell you this, if you please. When God takes the Prince in Kyiv, let the local princes – those of Volodymyr and Chernihiv, and Galicia, and Smolensk, and Polotsk, and Ryazan – assemble in Kyiv and, after giving it some thought, elect the most senior and worthy man and approve him by kissing the cross, the way it is done reasonably in other lands. The presence of the younger princes is not necessary; let them listen to these senior ones. And once the grand prince of the land of Rus has been elected, he should keep his oldest son in his homeland and portion out lands to the younger sons either there or in the land of Rus from Horyn and beyond the Dnipro, because cities there have been long gravitating towards Kyiv. If one of the brothers envies another and attacks a fellow brother's land, let the grand prince judge them with the local princes and get them to make peace. If the Cumans or Ugrians or Lachy or some other people mount an attack and a prince is unable to defend himself on his own, but only the grand price can, let him reach out to his brothers, local princes, who will send help from the entire land of Rus, as much as needed."

"To prevent the local princes from splintering, the principalities must not be divided among the sons, but instead the throne should be given to one oldest son together with the principality.

The younger ones should each be given a city or village to live off. And they must follow the orders of the older brother. If one does not have a son, it should be given to the blood brother. If one does not have a blood brother, it should be given to the most senior one of his clan so as not to splinter the force of Rus. It's good to stick together: when there were few princes in the land of Rus and they listened to the senior one, all the surrounding neighbors were fearful and respectful and did not dare go to war, which is what we see today. If you please, let us assemble in Kyiv and lay down the law after some thought..." [19].

This proposal can be considered a remarkable testimony to the political thought of our distant ancestors. If it had been adopted, decentralization trends in Rus would have been blocked. Unfortunately, this proposal met with opposition from Vsevolod the Big Nest, Prince of Vladimir-Suzdal, who wielded a great deal of power. Nor did it find support among the other Rus princes.

Prince Roman perished shortly after issuing his proposal. He was close to 50 years old at the time, leaving behind an enormous state that included Volhynia, Galicia, Podillia, Bucovina, and even the Kyiv region. It was arguably the biggest state formation in Europe. While Roman Mstyslavovych did not succeed in restoring the "old Rus", he created a "new" Rus. While previously the name "Rus" was applied mostly to the lands of Kyiv, now this usage was extended to most of what is now "right-bank Ukraine" (i.e., the territory west of the Dnipro river).

The political elite of the time also assumed that the Rus royal dynasty had "relocated" from Kyiv to Halych. Even the "Kyivan Synopsis" published in 1674 wrote about Roman Mstyslavovych that he "moved the throne of Kyiv statehood from Kyiv to Halych and presented himself as the ruler of all Rus". Note that this was written almost 470 years after Roman's passing. Memory about the "move of the throne" had been preserved for five centuries (!), but Russian historians simply "erased" the inconvenient truth that the rightful heir to the princely throne of Kyiv was Halych and not Moscow. [13]

The son of Roman Mstyslavovych – Danylo Romanovych Halytskyi – became the "king" and was the only one of the clan of the Rurikids to receive the crown and this European title from the Roman Pope (Pope Innocent IV) in 1253. After this the name "Kingdom of Ruthenia" applied to the Principality of Galicia–Volhynia and became generally recognized among European monarchs. Meanwhile, descendants of Prince Andrei Bogolyubsky and other Vladimir-Suzdal princes, starting from the mid-13th century, began receiving *yarlyk*, – permits that authorized them to rule their lands on behalf of the khan, collect tributes from their subject for the Mongol Tatars, and replicate their authoritarian and despotic Asian form of public governance.

Some of the aristocratic elite from the metropolis of the Rus Empire migrated first to the Principality of Galicia–Volhynia and eventually to the Grand Duchy of Lithuania and the Polish Kingdom. Some of them remained in the lands of Vladimir-Suzdal that would

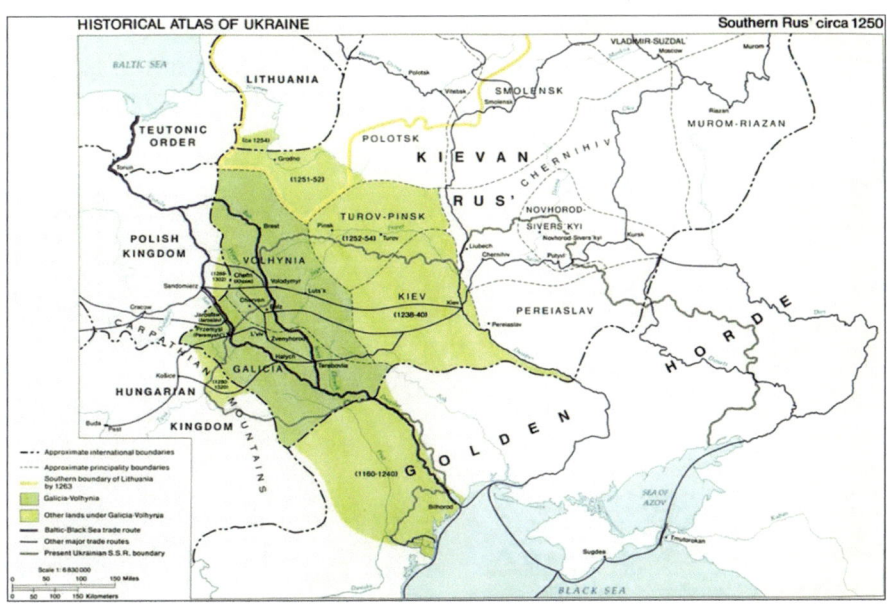

Principality of Galicia–Volhynia and lands subordinated to it. Illustration from the book by Paul Robert Magocsi, "History of Ukraine", Toronto, 1996
http://www.conflicts.rem33.com/images/Ukraine/halickarus_ukr.jpg

later become the homeland for the new "lands of Muscovy". In 1471 the "lands of Muscovy" were joined by the last northern bastion of the former vassal lands of the empire of the Rurikids – Velikiy Novgorod – complete with its freedom-loving system of European-style public self-governance, *veche* popular assemblies, church communities, and historical memory of the European grandeur of Kyiv with its Grand Prince and an elective ruler.

All of those rudiments of European democracy in the lands of Novgorod and Pskov were immediately destroyed. The Asian form of despotism would survive in Muscovy as it continued to pay tribute in accordance with the terms of a Tartar settlement.

One hundred years later, in 1571, Khan Devlet I Giray punished Muscovy for the last time by burning Moscow for coming up short with the tribute.

As regards more recent history, in response to all those who consider the name of the Ukrainian state to be "artificial", we direct them to an independent expert from the 18th century.

The following lines were written by a great Frenchman, Voltaire, who, at a time when Europe had not yet been accustomed to Muscovy's new name of "Russia" continues referring to it as "Muscovy".

Voltaire's History of Charles XII

    "Ukraine has always aspired to be free; but surrounded as she is by Muscovy, the states of the Grand Seignior [of Turkey], and Poland, she has been obliged to seek a protector, and consequently a master, in one of these three nations. First of all, she placed herself under the tutelage of Poland, which treated her too much like a dependency; then she gave herself to the Muscovite, who did his best to enslave her. To begin with, the Ukrainians enjoyed the privilege of electing a prince known as their hetman; but they were soon stripped of that right and their hetman was appointed by the Court of Moscow..." [2].

    To sum it up, modern-day Ukraine should draw lessons from the reasons for interruption of Rus-Ukraine's advancement towards European democracy in the 12th-13th centuries and later in the 17th and 20th centuries. The history of European democracies confirms

Image of Ivan Mazepa (smoking a pipe). Map of the German cartographer of the 18th century Johann Baptist Homann (1664-1724). Image is published on the website Vkraina.com – a unique collection of ancient European maps of Ukraine
*https://upload.wikimedia.org/wikipedia/commons/5/5c/Ukrania_quae_et_
Terra_Cosaccorum_cum_vicinis_Walachiae%2C_Moldoviae%2C_Johann_Baptiste_
Homann_%28Nuremberg%2C_1720%29.jpg*

59

that Ukraine cannot build a democratic European Ukraine without its own European-educated and cultured Ukrainian political elite, and without the revival of its own nationally-minded, primarily military aristocracy as a guarantor of consistency and state-building continuity. Efforts to formulate a contemporary national idea and strategy for Ukraine's development should be combined with the revival of the type of national elites that would willingly assume responsibility for Ukraine.

The Ukrainian Cossack State. Europeanization and modernization of Muscovy

Ukrainian Cossack state under the 1649 Treaty of Zboriv.
https://forhistory.xyz/testi-natsionalno-vizvolna-vijna/

In 1991, after the West won the Cold War against the Soviet Union and the latter collapsed, Ukraine became an independent state once again in its recent history.

The Cossack state of Ukraine – the direct descendant of the medieval European state of Rus with its capital in ancient Kyiv – gained its independence for the first time back in the mid-17th century. The first mention of the name "Ukraine" appears in the Kyivan Chronicle of the Hypatian Codex dated 1187 and presumably derives from the Slavic word for a "separate, clannish country" [22].

After the destruction and plundering of Kyiv by the first "Russian" state, and the second and even worse devastation unleashed on the lands of Kyivan Rus by Mongols, Ukraine entered a period of great ruination between the 13th and 15th centuries. Muscovy avoided such ruination because its rulers submitted to the Mongols and accepted vassalage until 1480 in order to preserve their power over their subjects.

Despite the damage inflicted on Kyiv by the early Russian (i.e. Muscovite) state, Ukrainians proved to be better neighbors towards Russians centuries later in the aftermath of several disastrous wars between the Russians and the Rzeczpospolita (the Polish-Lithuanian Commonwealth). As early as 1610, the Russian state was on the verge of losing its independence when its capital, Moscow, was

Illustration from the article titled "Defeat of the Polish Army in the Battle of Zboriv" published on the "Military Review" website. The map shows the borders of the Cossack state (the Hetmanate) under the 1649 Treaty of Zboriv, under the 1651 Treaty of Bila Tserkva (after the defeat in the Battle of Berestechko), as well as the territory that went to Muscovy under the 1667 Truce of Andrusovo.
https://topwar.ru/161102-porazhenie-polskoj-armii-pod-zborovom.html

conquered and occupied by Commonwealth forces and the majority of Moscow citizens and almost all local aristocrats swore an oath of allegiance to Prince Władysław, son of the King of Poland and Sigismund III, Grand Duke of Lithuania. They refer to this period as the "Time of Troubles".

Concurrently and with notably contrasting results, Ukrainian Cossacks defeated the forces of the Polish king in their 6-year war of independence and, by 1654, restored Ukraine's statehood without any assistance from its "younger (Muscovite) brother". In breaking away from the Rzeczpospolita, and entering into a military alliance with Muscovy, Ukraine strategically weakened Muscovy's biggest western enemy since the 15th century. Its intervention provided Russia – now free of its eastern (Mongolian) and western enemies – with a second opportunity to change its evolutionary path and "reboot" its trajectory towards Europe.

Many historians consider this military alliance with Muscovy (the Pereyaslav Agreement) to have been a mistake and a great tragedy in that it not only weakened the western powers threatening Muscovy but also provided Muscovy's Czar with the opportunity to meddle in the affairs of the Cossack state and to introduce troops, under the guise of "protective garrisons" in a number of Ukrainian towns. It is also the basis for Russia's continuing claim of "unification" between the two nations. However, it was common practice at the time to enter military alliances between heads of state but without any presumption of "union". The Cossacks treated the agreement as simply an enhancement of their position in common defense of "Orthodoxy" with the Czar of Muscovy against a Catholic Rzeczpospolita and a Muslim Turkish Ottaman, while the Czar saw it as an opportunity to expand his influence and power. The details of the treaty – whether it was to be a military union, or make a commonwealth with Ukraine, or completely incorporate it into the Tsardom of Russia – are uncertain, as the original final text has not survived. Translations and drafts of some articles show the wording to have been vague. But, regardless, the unfortunate reality is that this agreement opened the door to 350 years of Russian occupation and colonization of Ukraine with all its consequential tragedies.

In the aftermath of the agreement, Ukraine not only failed to strengthen its own position but it strategically reinforced Muscovy's defenses in the West, and guarded "with her own body" Muscovy's southern borders with the Turkish Empire and the Crimean Khanate to which Muscovy had been paying tributes until 1700. But most importantly, yet again Ukraine supplied Muscovy with the decisive cultural, human, materiel, and military potential which Muscovy used to its advantage to officially declare itself the "Russian empire" in 1721. All the while it hijacked not only the millennium-long purely European history of ancient Kyivan Rus but also the very historical name of the state.....perhaps the first historical case of deliberate identity-theft by a nation.

It may be instructive for the reader to consider Ukrainian and Russian trajectories, during the course of the 15th, 16th, and the first half of the 17th century, through the "eyes" of a descendant of one of the oldest noble families of Russia – the Trubetskoys:

"The culture of western Rus (Ukraine) and the culture of Moscow Rus evolved along such different paths, that by the mid-17th century the difference between those two cultures became abysmal... After the annexation of Ukraine, it came time to merge these two versions of the Rus culture together...

"... Ukrainians considered the Muscovite version of the Rus culture to be corrupted because of the illiteracy of Muscovites, and reproached them for their lack of schools, and boasted before them of how well they run their schools. Meanwhile, Muscovites believed the Ukrainian (and generally western Rus) version of the Rus culture to be corrupted as a result of the... Latin-Polish influence.

"... The government sided with Ukrainians, which was an absolutely correct thing to do from the political standpoint: the inevitable dissatisfaction of Greater Russians could have at most escalated in riots of a purely local nature, whereas the dissatisfaction of Ukrainians could significantly complicate or even render impossible any true reunion of Ukraine...

"... Czar Peter made it his mission to Europeanize Russian culture. Obviously, only the Western Rus (Ukrainian) version of the Rus culture was suitable for this task, as it had already absorbed some of the elements of the European culture (as represented by the Polish version of that culture) and manifested a trend towards a continued evolution in the same direction. On the contrary, the Greater Russian version of the Rus culture was not only unfit for Peter's purposes but also directly interfered with the accomplishment of this mission as a result of its pronounced europhobia and self-importance. Peter therefore did his best to completely eradicate and destroy this Great Russian version of the Rus culture, and made the Ukrainian culture the single version of the Rus culture serving as a starting point for a continued evolution..." [20].

As the Mongol Empire receded, another empire – that of Turkey with its Tartar allies – rose to take its place. It is important to understand what had been happening during the intervening period (prior to the break-up of the Rzeczpospolita by Ukrainian Cossacks) and, especially the impact of the two empires on Muscovy and the rebirth of the Ukrainian state in the form of the Cossack brotherhood.

First and foremost, these two empires played a major role in the emergence of Ukrainian Cossacks as ancestors of contemporary Ukrainians. The Cossacks restored Ukrainian statehood in the form of a Cossack state in the mid-17th century (a time when a contemporary and united Germany or Italy had not yet emerged, while France and England were still torn apart by civil wars).

Here is what the late 19th century historians of the Austro-Hungarian and Russian empires wrote about the emergent independent Ukraine: "After the Tatars raided Kyiv and subjugated Rus, new political centers formed in Moscow on the one hand and in Lithuania on the other; any political and cultural life had ground to a standstill in Kyiv during this time. The country was becoming increasingly emptier: those who were spared by Tatar weapons had been taken captive or moved out; and those few people, who stayed behind, lived in constant danger and grew wild after running for their lives into the woods and swamps.....Then free communities arose. Since the 15th century, they became known as "Cossacks".

"Already in the 15th century, there were many people previously ravaged by Tatars in the no-man's land along the Dnipro. They were running away from unbearable oppression in Poland and Muscovy... and they quickly earned recognition as a Christian stronghold against the Tatars. They were a skillful and militant people who only needed military organization to become a formidable force. Stefan Bathory (Polish King, 1576-1586) was the first to notice this class in the interests of his country and compiled a register of battle-worthy fighters, initially limiting their number to 600. In doing so, he secured fresh forces for his country against Russia (Muscovy)..."

"Under Sigismund III, the Sejm ruled in 1590 to keep 6,000 Cossacks on payroll. They were added to the register and called "registered Cossacks"...

"Registered Cossacks owned land. They had their own court in Baturyn and freely elected their leaders. All other Cossacks (an incomparably overwhelming majority) had to return back to being peasants... Yet the Polish nobles were reluctant to admit even those 6,000 into their environment... This provoked strife. Registered Cossacks united with the unregistered ones and rose against the government... What business did free Cossacks have getting involved in Poland's state interests? Above all else they loved freedom and war, and went to war gladly as if to a banquet. Often rivaling the daring Varangians, they would go down the Dnipro in their small chaika boats to the Black Sea and raided the outskirts of Constantinople or the cities of Kilia, Akerman, Izmayil, Sinop, and others..."

"Danhkevych – the leader of the Cherkasy Cossacks on the Dnipro – traveled to Poland with a demand for the Sejm to recognize the free detachments as an official state army tasked with protecting the borders (of the Rzeczpospolita)... But this did not happen, so when the government decided to limit the freedom of the Cossacks' movement, they went beyond the rapids south of the city of Cherkasy. The free Cossack army congregated here and was no longer ruled by any duke.

The first mention of this Zaporozhian Sich (an administrative unit that literally translates as "a forest clearing" of "Cossacks beyond the rapids") appears in a 1568 letter of King Sigismund II Augustus... Their strongholds were Tomakivka, Khortytsia, Bazavluk, Chortomlyk, and other places where they had reinforcements.

They organized similarly to a Western European order of knights. Unconditional disciplines, piety, virtuous conduct in the camp, complete equality of everyone were conditions of daily life in the Sich. The general assembly (circle) was the only governance. They elected leaders: the hetman, who performed his duties for only one year, after which he could be held accountable for his activities and even sentenced to execution; captains who served as lower military chiefs; and the scribe. The assembly was the only judiciary. Fights were strictly prohibited. Theft and robberies of Christians were punishable by death... Cossacks lived by the laws of the Orthodox Church and strictly observed lent. Their principal mission was fighting the infidels.

This marked the beginning of a successful development of a new institution; it even seemed as if a new state was emerging based on new, non-European values (in contrast to the absolute rule of monarchies in Europe at the time). While Poland and the rest of Europe acknowledged and cared about the freedom of only selected social classes, among Cossacks even the lowest classes demanded the same amount of freedom. Moreover, no classes whatsoever were supposed to exist there other than a free people. ... Everything gravitated towards the Sich, which had become a crystallizing point in Ukraine... The Cossack life was shrouded in a romantic aura... It seemed as if this Lesser Rus tribe was destined to make the dream of universal equality and freedom a reality. The art of combat was also practiced to perfection here. They also created their own literature that glorified the life of Cossacks in exciting songs and tales. Indeed, the entire Slavdom could be proud of this free state.

... Cossacks could have brought unfathomable benefits for their country (Ukraine – Auth.) and the entire state if Poland managed to give this new entity a worthy place within the state machinery. However, democratic Cossacks were unfit for the nobility state. Three starkly segregated classes existed in Poland and Lithuania after the Union of Lublin (*in 1569, the Polish Crown and the Grand Duchy of Lithuania united to form a single state – the Rzeczpospolita of the two peoples – Auth.*): nobility, city residents, and bonded peasants. There was no place for Cossacks among those three classes…

Cossacks had such a strong magnetic influence on the peasant class of Poland and Lithuania that only the cruelest penalties could keep the folk from escaping to Ukraine en masse… The economic might of the Polish nobility state relied on the serfdom of the rural population… That is why the nobles were driven by a mortal hatred in persecuting Cossacks – former peasants who had the audacity to position themselves as their equals. Since the abyss between them could not be bridged, the conflict became inevitable…" [6].

Yet even the brief appearance of the Ukrainian Cossack state on the world's map one hundred years before the United States began its fight for independence (1775-1783) fundamentally changed the strategic balance of forces in Europe and eventually in the world.

As a result of the Ukrainian people's struggle in 1648-1654 against attempts at total subjugation and Polonization by the-then largest European state – the Rzeczpospolita (the territory of what are now Poland, Lithuania, Ukraine, and Belarus) – the latter was strategically weakened. Just one year after Ukraine separated from it in 1654, much of Poland with both its new and old capitals (Krakow and Warsaw) was temporarily conquered by Swedes in 1655. While the Rzeczpospolita continued to play an important role in European politics for some time afterwards, having lost most of Ukraine's human and natural resources, it became too vulnerable to the newly created Russian empire in 1721. Between 1772 and 1795 the Rzeczpospolita was divided among Russia, Austria, and Prussia and Poland did not regain its independence until 1918.

Ukrainian Cossacks, having had the poor judgment and great misfortune of allying themselves in 1654 with a predominantly

Asian (in terms of culture and governance) Muscovite ruler, laid the groundwork for Europeanization and modernization of Muscovy by reinforcing it with its cultural, human, and material resources [20]. They effectively guarded the weak southwestern borders of Muscovy, while simultaneously inflicting a fatal wound on Muscovy's biggest enemy of the time – the Rzeczpospolita. Shortly afterwards Muscovy appropriated for itself the three centuries of history and cultural heritage of the entire ancient Rus state.

The direct descendants of "Ruthenian people"(i.e. Ukrainians), whose ancestors once brought the Christian faith and underlying principles of statehood to Muscovy – had been renamed in the new empire as "Little Russians". Relatively weak by European standards, Muscovy gradually grew into a powerful Eurasian empire.

The Cossack Constitution.
The unlearned lessons of the Hetmanate and the national idea of Ukraine

Modern constitutional monarchies of the UK, Sweden, Norway, Denmark, Belgium, the Netherlands, Spain, and Japan are among the most successful democracies in the world. These countries have an effective separation of the three branches of power into legislative, executive, and judiciary, which are truly independent of one another. They have an effective electoral system with multi-party politics, while the rule of law and high standards of living are protected by effective laws.

Although the monarchs of these countries have the status of heads of state whose rights and duties are normally outlined in the constitution, they primarily serve as moral authorities, the embodiment of established national and historical traditions, guarantors of rights and freedoms of their people, and the ultimate unifying

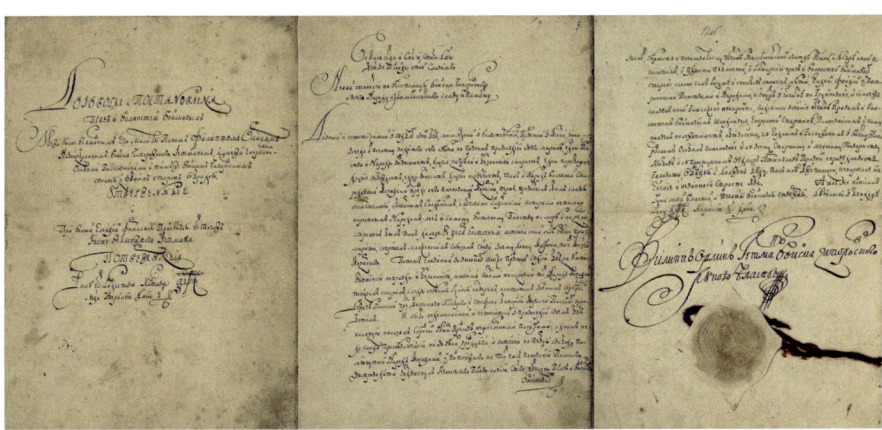

The Treaties and Resolutions of the Rights and Freedoms of the Zaporozhian Army ("Pylyp Orlyk's Constitution"). 1710

voices and bulwarks in times of distress for the stability of the nation.

One of Europe's oldest constitutions – *The Treaties and Resolutions of the Rights and Freedoms of the Zaporozhian Army* ("Philip Orlyk's Constitution") – written in 1710 (77 years before the adoption of the U.S. Constitution), already limited the rights of an elected Ukrainian "hetman" (head of state) and introduced the democratic principle of separation of power into legislative, executive, and judicial branches.

Under this Constitution, the legislative power in the Cossack State of Ukraine was vested in the General Council that acted as a parliament and was to meet in sessions three times a year: in January (on Christmas Day), in April (on Easter Day), and in October (on Holy Protection Day). The Council was tasked with addressing issues of foreign and domestic policy and national security; hearing the hetman's reports (including possible votes of no confidence); and electing the hetman's government, the general officer staff, nominated by him.

The executive branch of power was headed by the hetman himself, who was elected for a lifetime term but could be dismissed prematurely by a decision of the General Council. Funding for the hetman's activities, including the allocation of "rank estates", was limited to his term in office. The judiciary branch was independent from the hetman and limited the hetman's rights in managing the state treasury and lands, and prohibited him from conducting an independent foreign and staffing policy, as well as attempting to create his own administration.

According to an 1896 assessment by leading historians of the Austro-Hungarian and Russian empire, Ukrainian "democratic Cossacks" set an example for Europe as early as the 16th – 17th centuries of a new state operating on principles that were "the most democratic" on the continent at the time [6].

Unfortunately, the first state established by Ukrainian "democratic Cossacks" of the 17th century had very little opportunity to evolve while surrounded and blocked by authoritarian countries during "the rule of absolute monarchies" in Europe.

First, the social and economic stability and military might of the Cossack state could grow only on condition of a growing Ukrainian middle class, i.e., the registered Cossacks and emancipated peasants. The latter dreamed of being free farmers or artisans. They were the ones who formed the primary reserve of people who, if need be, were ready to fight for the independence of Ukraine and join the ranks of its free fighters – the Cossacks.

The Ukrainian people's natural striving for freedom, a fair distribution of land, and land ownership, which fueled the growth of the Cossack army, almost immediately clashed with the interests of a large group of self-enamored and egotistical Cossack commanders. After Ukraine signed a union treaty with Muscovy in 1654, this popular sentiment caused additional friction with the interests of the Muscovite czar and his serf-owning feudal system. The Rzeczpospolita, the Ottoman Empire, and Muscovy were interested in using the vast potential of the Cossacks – a community of some of the best professional warriors in Europe – to fight external enemies and protect their borders. At the same time these nations were categorically opposed to the spread of the democratic customs and traditions of the Cossacks within their own states and lands subordinated to them. The example of the freedom-loving Cossacks of Ukraine was a direct threat to their despotic and authoritarian forms of public governance and serfdom, which was tantamount to slavery.

Second, the absolute monarchy of Muscovy gladly welcomed and took advantage of the civilizational and cultural mission of Ukraine for its own modernization and partial Europeanization. Yet the form of this civilizational and cultural modernization of the gigantic Eurasian expanses differed substantially from Western Europe's expansion with respect to the countries of the Americas, Asia, and Africa.

Western countries had not only a higher level of civilizational and cultural development compared to the colonies dependent on them, but also much stronger agencies of public government and their own armies. In exchange for progressive influence on the colonized peoples, the colonizers used their human and natural re-

sources for their own enrichment, improvement of their own econ-
omies, and growth of a domestic middle class.

In stark contrast to west European colonial experience, Ukraine
was the more advanced civilization and culture. Ukraine surren-
dered to Muscovy its entire best civilizational and cultural heritage
but received nothing in return. It provided Muscovy its highly-edu-
cated human resources in science, education, and administration,
and who later became the most active builders and administrators
of the future Russian empire. Some notable names include: The-
ophan Prokopovich, an ideologue and reformer under Peter I; Stefan Yavorsky, archbishop and the first president of the Most Holy
Synod; grand chancellors – Alexander Bezborodko (1747–1799) and
Viktor Kochubey (1768–1834), as well as other high-ranking imperial
officials – the Rozumovskys, Hudovychs, Zavydovskys, Troshchyn-
skys, Myloradovychs, to name just a few.

Gradually, over the course of one and a half century, Ukraine
was not only forced to surrender its best human, natural, and military resources to Muscovy, but also irrevocably lost the remnants
of its own original autonomy and rudiments of a state democracy.
Muscovy forced on Ukraine its authoritarian autocratic system of
government with slavery for peasants and the absence of independent branches of government. In doing so it canceled the election
of the hetman and Cossack commanders, abolished the Zaporozhian Sich and the register of Cossacks, and introduced mass serfdom for heretofore free peasants and the majority of free Cossacks.

The lack of an aristocratic, nationally-minded, and cultured
political elite in Ukraine at the time was one of the primary reasons for this tragic reversal in the further development of Ukraine's
fledgling democracy. For over three centuries it put the brakes on
Ukraine's natural social and political advancement towards Europe.

The most recent attempt at building an Ukrainian hetman
state was in 1918. Hetman Pavlo Skoropadskyi was head of state
for about eight months: from April to December 1918. His Hetman
State became the most successful Ukrainian state formation during
the period of the 1917-1920 revolution. The months of Pavlo Skoro-

padskyi's rule brought Ukraine a comparatively stable existence despite the surrounding turmoil of the civil war and the culmination of World War I.

Ukrainian maps such as the one above dated 1918 were purposefully destroyed and those caught in possession of one could face 10 years in jail.

Historical map of the Ukrainian State under Hetman Pavlo Skoropadskyi as of October 1918, published in Vienna in 1918 by the famous cartographic company Freytag & Berndt (stored in Lviv History Museum; another copy of the map has been found in Vancouver: https:// ukrainianvancouver. com/1918-map-of-ukraine-found-in-vancouver/). The contemporary border of Ukraine is highlighted in blue on the map. Interesting facts: 1) The Ukrainian People's Republic did not yet include the West Ukrainian People's Republic, which was proclaimed on November 1—after the map had been printed; 2) The Ukrainian state included the territory of Transnistria, part of Belarus—Berestia, Gomel region (80-150 km into Belarus), part of Russia— Starodubshchyna (up to 120 km into Russia) and eastern Slobozhanshchyna (up to 250 km into Russia: modern-day Kursk and Voronezh Regions), as well as Crimea (the army of the Ukrainian People's Republic liberated Crimea from the Bolsheviks and established control over the Black Sea Navy; however, Germany was dissatisfied with this, and the Ukrainian army soon pulled out of Crimea); 3) In February 1918, the Legislative Council of the Independent Kuban People's Republic passed a resolution on the annexation of Kuban to Ukraine; however, Kuban existed as part of the Ukrainian People's Republic for only a few months. (http://history.sumy.ua/maps-and-plans/389-kartaukrajinskojiderzhavapavlaskorop adskogo1918r.html)

Pavlo Skoropadskyi. Source: Wikimedia Commons
https://upload.wikimedia.org/wikipedia/commons/5/52/Pavlo_Skoropadsky.jpg

Born in Ukraine and educated as an imperial guard officer, Pavlo Skoropadskyi managed to accomplish a great deal for Ukraine in a short time. He put the economy back on track and restored its administrative machinery; introduced a national currency and stabilized the financial system; reopened Ukrainian schools, universities, and theaters; recreated the National Academy of Sciences and set up the National Archives and Library from scratch.

Skoropadskyi was made Hetman of Ukraine by the Germans in the aftermath of the Treaty of Brest Litovsk which provided Ukraine with military support against Russia. However, the presence of Central Power (German and Austro-Hungarian) troops was viewed by Ukrainians as enabling occupation. Notwithstanding those popular sentiments, Skoropadskyi recognized the opportunities it offered for building an independent Ukrainian state, and often acted contrary to the wishes of his foreign sponsors. He started by laying the foundation for a regular professional Ukrainian army in line with historical Cossack traditions. Despite German resistance he anticipated assembling a 300,000 strong regular Ukrainian army by the spring of 1919 but failed to meet his goal when forced to abdicate in December 1918 by politically ambitious opponents.

And yet, despite his many accomplishments during his brief 8-month tenure as head of state, Pavlo Skoropadskyi – a brilliant hereditary aristocrat, a combat general of the imperial army with a classical education and a vast cultural worldview—proved unable to rally the majority of the Ukrainian people to support his plans to build a hetman state that he envisioned as a law-governed democratic and sovereign state with elements of constitutional "monarchy" after the fashion of modern-day Britain or Sweden. However, unlike the monarchies of Europe, the Hetmanate in Ukraine had never been envisaged as a hereditary monarchy. Voltaire, himself, in his *History of Charles XII* published in 1730. Pointed out the Ukrainians' democratic principle of having an elected hetman...

Pavlo Skoropadskyi viewed Russian Bolshevism as the biggest enemy of Ukrainian independence. He believed that only a strong and nationally cohesive state was capable of stopping it. It had to be built upon: a strong army and professional state machinery; a stable economy with an emphasis on education; a manufacturing industry and agriculture as well as a revived national culture, law and order. The Hetman's principal mottoes were: "law and order", "inviolability of private property", "calm and creative work".

Any construction (including state-building) requires three underlying elements. First, a gifted and experienced chief architect who has to come up with the idea and design for construction. Second, a team of qualified managers, engineers, and skilled builders those are capable of bringing this project to life. Third, a sufficient quantity and quality of construction materials needed to complete the construction project.

In the building of a state the corresponding elements would include first the leader of the state with his idea ("architectural design of state-building"); second, a ruling political elite capable of making strategic decisions and adjustments and implementing it together with the leader, and third, an appropriate social base in the country that has to support the proposed project and construction plan.

While the state-building plan is being implemented, this social base must be transformed into a critical mass of nationally-minded citizens who will rise to defend the country against external and internal enemies whenever a threat arises. To better understand the conditions in which Pavlo Skoropadskyi, the chief architect of the third Hetman State, was forced to work, let us compare these conditions with the conditions in which another architect of national independence – that of Finland -Baron Carl Gustaf Emil Mannerheim worked. A brother-in-arms of Pavlo Skoropadskyi in WWI, as well as a general of the Russian imperial army, Carl Mannerheim became the most outstanding military and government official in 20th century Finland.

At the time when it proclaimed its independence from the Russian Empire in 1917, Finland (unlike Ukraine) already had its own Constitution (since 1809) and vast domestic and external autonomy. This facilitated the evolutionary growth of the country's own

Pavlo Petrovych Skoropadskyi and Carl Gustaf Emil Mannerheim (source: Wikimedia Commons). Two generals of the Russian imperial army. The Ukrainian is almost 6 years his junior, but they earned their military ranks almost at the same time: Skoropadsky was promoted to cornet one year later than Mannerheim; to Stabsrittmeister – two years later; to colonel – one year later; to major general – also one year later (however, they were added to His Imperial Majesty's Retinue at the same time). Skoropadskyi rose to the rank of Lieutenant General in 1916, while Mannerheim did so one year later.

nationally-minded middle class as well as stable political and legal democratic traditions among the political elite of the time – the intelligentsia. The new Finnish leader managed to find almost immediately an appropriate social base to support his efforts. The Finnish middle class- a union of the intelligentsia and peasants – became this social base.

Another factor at play was that when the Finnish Senate instructed Baron Mannerheim to create a national army as a way to ward off the threat of the country's "Bolshevization", he immediately received support from Germany. But in Ukraine, the German occupation administration blocked the same efforts by Hetman Pavlo Skoropadskyi until almost the very end. Skoropadskyi often gets compared with Mannerheim and reproached for having underestimated the role of minor landowners in Ukraine while supporting mostly large landowners. This is not quite true. The land issue was indeed a big challenge for the Hetman. He simply ran out of time and could not find enough competent assistants to bring his plans to fruition. Skoropadskyi was not a revolutionary and genuinely believed in the force of law. He believed that land had to be transferred from large landowners and distributed to smaller farmers but only through a multi-year buyout procedure made possible by state guarantees. The Hetman did not believe that simply confiscating private property could create a new and effective user of such property.

He also wanted to see Ukraine as a country of small and medium, privately owned, highly productive enterprises like those he saw before the start of the war in Europe and Ukraine in the wake of Stolypin's land reforms.

"Late at night we reached some hamlet 10 miles off Novohrad-Volynsky," the Hetman wrote in his *Memoirs*: "In the village hut I spoke to the owners. They were peasant proprietors of the Stolypin reform. Early in the morning I joined them on a tour of the entire hamlet, and I was thrilled with what I saw. I have never seen such order and wealth in a peasant farm, even though I traveled and stayed for a long time among peasants, especially during the war. The peasant proprietors attributed their prosperity to the fact that they had been divided up into peasant proprietorships). The host kept adding: 'Yes, now it's worth working. Nothing will be lost. We don't have to explain anything to anyone'..." [18].

Pavlo Skoropadskyi was ahead of his time in terms of his overall level of culture and worldview compared to the majority of political forces and social groups in Ukraine; he simply ran out of time before he could rally an appropriate political and social base around him to support his state-building project.

"I was surprised to learn that only socialist parties existed. And if they could do something, it was in a field completely unrelated to the conditions we had at hand. ... Looking at the complete disorientation that existed among all colors of more or less wealthy classes, it seemed to me that we only had Ukrainian social democrats and Ukrainian social revolutionaries, and the others were an undefined popular mass...

"Over the course of ten months, through constant communication with specific representatives of these parties, I became convinced that despite their sincerity and willingness to create something, they were intellectually incapable of putting the country on a progressive path... All of these thoughts brought me to an understanding that I needed to form a democratic party as a matter of obligation (a Ukrainian is a democrat at heart), but in no case should it be a socialist party. Further, this party should preach Ukrainianism, but not the extreme chauvinistic kind. It should clearly focus on the development of the Ukrainian culture without touching or cultivating hatred of all things Russian.

"I believed that a party like this would unite all owners regardless of their colors in a fight against destructive socialist slogans... Foreigners do not understand this about us; they think that we can stay on the course of reasonable socialism, the way this happens in western countries. I am deeply convinced that this is impossible in our country. If the government chooses to support our socialist parties, it will rapidly slide into extreme Bolshevism. I consider this an axiom.

First we must democratize the country, educate people, instill in them a sense of duty, integrity, broaden their cultural worldview, and only then can we begin discussing the next stage of the socialist revolution... I thought that the party which I attempted to create would lead those on the right and on the left to a middle ground in terms of social policy, in terms of the Greater Russian and Ukrainian issues in the nationalistic sense...[8]

Yet even the inner circle of the Hetman proved unable to help transform his thoughts and plans into political slogans understandable to the majority of Ukrainians – the ideological blueprint for construction of the new State. In other words, they needed new simple slogans understandable to Ukrainians – ideas that could become a new national idea of Ukraine. "Without a doubt, creating an army is a good thing, but it takes time. But more importantly, in creating an army, what kind of slogans could I propose? Under the czarist regime, the slogan was: the czar, the faith, the motherland. The only slogan understandable to peasants is land. As for freedom, they lost faith themselves for some reason, but still, they want all of the land" [18].

Given the political struggle against mass socialization of the population, only a new national idea spread through a new democratic party and perceived by the majority of the Ukrainian people would have been able to unite both Ukraine's west and east around the Hetman. An appropriate social base would have been created to support his state-building efforts and stop the spread of populist slogans that are damaging to Ukraine's independence and are alien to Ukraine:

"Land for peasants!", "Plants and factories for workers!",

"War for palaces", "All power for Soviets".

Similar political slogans were supported at the time by Mykhailo Hrushevskyi, Ukrainian socialists-revolutionaries, and such social democrats as Mykyta Shapoval, Symon Petliura, and Volodymyr Vynnychenko. The latter even put forth an ultimatum: either a socialist Ukraine or no Ukraine. A large number of Ukrainians, bewildered by the war and the revolution, were becoming increasingly mesmerized by these slogans. They would almost inevitably bring Russian Bolsheviks to power in Ukraine.

Viacheslav Lypynskyi described the need to formulate a new national idea of Ukraine as follows: "Since we have both the east and the west in our nation, we must harmonize these two aspects at all times under a motto proclaiming the unity of our national identity. Without such harmonization we are dying as a nation: we find ourselves influenced by either Moscow or Western Poland without having been conquered by foreign arms, but always conquered by our internal beliefs [12].

In his *Letters to Brother Grain Growers*, Lypynskyi emphasizes the great significance of, and need for, synthesizing a similar unifying idea with a transition from a simplified national parochial mentality to the formulation of the ideals of our "Ukrainian Messianism…"

However, the lack of genuine culture and a vast worldview, the primitive parochial mentality, and the narcissism of the majority of the political elite of the time did not allow it to transcend the slogans: "Land for peasants!" and "Plants and factories for workers!". They were even incapable of realizing that these slogans are a good weapon only for seizing power but absolutely useless for retaining it.

Having used these slogans to initially seize power in Russia, the Bolsheviks even toyed with the idea of "Ukrainizing" the cultural life Soviet Ukraine. Later on, having gained strength, the repressive machinery of the new empire destroyed the nationally-minded Ukrainian intelligentsia and proclaimed "Ukrainian bourgeois nationalism" to be one of its primary ideological targets for decades.

The man-made famine of 1932-1993 claimed millions of lives of working peasants — both small and medium land owners as a class in Ukraine. Any surviving peasants were forced into the serfdom of the new "socialist agriculture". The social base which Skoropadskyi thought was needed to resist Bolshevism in Ukraine was destroyed for years to come.

Unlike Petliura and Vynnychenko, Pavlo Skoropadskyi anticipated this course of events in Ukraine many years in advance. "I have no doubt, like I had no doubt before, that all sorts of socialist experiments under a socialist government scenario would immediately cause the entire country to fall prey to the all-encompassing evil of Bolshevism over the course of six weeks. After destroying all kinds of culture, Bolshevism would turn our country into a parched desert where capitalism would take root over time. But what kind of capitalism! Not the weak and soft-bodied capitalism that has been emerging here up till now, but an all-powerful god at whose feet the same people would slither" [18].

Does this not remind you of modern-day Ukraine where new "all-powerful gods" have replaced the powerful gods of Bolshevism and have emerged to play a much bigger role in the country's social and political life than they did a century ago? The fact that Ukraine lacks genuine national aristocrats and political elite is one of the biggest challenges for successful national state-building.

In this context, the open letter of Colonel Petro Bolbochan (another notable representative of the military aristocracy) to Symon Petliura, (who led the coup against Skoropadskyi) is extremely telltale. In his letter published on January 26, 1919, the hero of the fight against Bolshevism in eastern Ukraine and in Crimea underscores:

"Poor Ukraine, we are fighting Bolshevism. The entire cultural world has risen to fight it, and the newly appointed Ukrainian government of the Ukrainian People's Republic is heading towards Bolshevism and Bolsheviks! You can't even sort out the most basic issues of life, but still you are hell-bent on becoming ministers, otamans, leaders of a great state, and legislators, instead of serving as the most basic government officials and secretaries".

Shortly after publishing it, Colonel Bolbochan—was arrested on orders from Petliura, tortured and executed by firing squad that same year.

In April 1934, during a special session of the Society of Ukrainian Lawyers and the Society of Zaporozhian Cossacks who met in Prague to study the reason for the execution of Colonel Bolbochan, social democrat B. Martos (former head of the Ukrainian government and fellow party member of Symon Petliura) offered the following reasoning for the government's decision to execute him: "You ask me: Why was Bolbochan executed? Imagine a dandy—clean-shaven, powdered, perfumed, in lacquered boots, epaulets? Is that a Ukrainian military commander? That's a genuine reactionary. Imagine what would happen to us if his reactionary ideas prevailed. He needed to be executed, so we executed him..." [17].

"If they, meaning the Directorate, do not come to their senses, but instead fire all Russian officials again and install their illiterate young men in their places, this will result in chaos that's no better than what they had under the Central Council. When I said: Wait up,

Petro Bolbochan and Symon Petliura (source: Wikimedia Commons). Isn't it puzzling: Why does the name of one and the same essentially bad person has a different negative meaning for different peoples?

do not rush things: create your own intelligentsia, your own specialists in all sector of public governance, they immediately became defensive and said: 'This is impossible'...

"From a social perspective, the Galicians exhibit greater moderation. They are not even socialists, but simply democratically-minded people. In this sense they could be very useful for us; they would contain the zeal of our intelligentsia raised in Russian schools with all of their negative traits (*authoritarianism – Auth.*).

".. Further, there is one more trait, but it applies to many political figures (*those in power in Kyiv – Auth.*) — lack of principles and complete absence of chivalry. They complained that the old regime had been stealing; however, it is unimaginable by how much this phenomenon has grown now during the revolution." [18].

It is only natural that similar pseudo-political elites were incapable of—and did not even preoccupy themselves with—formulating a new national idea of Ukraine that would be consistent with the vision of the highest spiritual, socioeconomic, and state-building values of the Ukrainian people..... values that could have united both the west and the east of Ukraine and lay the groundwork for formulating a national development strategy of Ukraine that would be understandable to not just Ukrainians but also the rest of the world.

But is this question all that important and relevant for the Ukrainians today, one hundred years after the Third Hetmanate? Have we considered the mistakes of the past and elaborated our own new vision based on modern familiarity of the world? After all, nations form not on their own but under the influence of their own national elites.

From whom did contemporary Ukraine inherit its heritage? In answering this question, Prof. Yuri Tereshchenko, Ph.D. outlined the problem as follows:

"If you consider what Kravchuk (first president of Ukraine after the country regained its independence) did, he took over the heritage of the Ukrainian National Republic... If we want to recreate the Hetman State, we must take a whole series of steps: First: transform our sociopolitical system and restore the Third Hetmanate. But this is only step one. Do we need to know what we want ideologically? Oligarchs have come to power. How do we return to civilization? We have to change the situation drastically. How we should do it—that's the question..."

Humanity's historical experience shows that there were and still are peoples and nations that did not and do not have any formalized ideas and strategies of their own national development, which would be understood by the majority of the population. Marx and Engels categorized them as "non-state peoples". Such peoples and nations exist to this day. However, the same historical experience indicates that, first, such peoples never succeeded in shaping their own destiny; and, second, the impact of such peoples on both their own progressive development and that of mankind was historically minimal. "Sleeping people", as Kemal Atatürk called them, "either vanish or wake up enslaved".

The history of mankind also proves that it is the national idea that reflects the history of a particular nation and its characteristics and uniqueness among the nations of the world. It actually defines the mission of a nation's existence at specific critical stages of its development. Self-awareness, purpose, and the sense of existence of any successful nation or people create preconditions for their continued progressive evolution. In our case, according to Lypynskyi, the national idea has to define the path of development of "Ukrainian Messianism".

For example, the history of modern European civilization is unimaginable without its impact on the development of peoples and nations that at different times were guided and united by their own national ideas, thus becoming active creators of history:

"*SPQR: Senatus Populusque Romanus* – the Roman Senate and People" [rule Rome];

"Culture and agriculture will forever feed France";

"Britain is the ruler of the seas!";

"Freedom, Equality, Brotherhood!";

"All people are created equal and have been vested by the Creator with certain inalienable rights to life, freedom and pursuit of happiness";

"One God, one fatherland. Germany above all!";

"Renaissance! We have created Italy; it only remains to create the Italian people!";

"Honor and Fatherland! Poland is not yet lost!";

"Orthodoxy, Monarchy, Ethnicity";

"Proletarians of all countries—unite!";

"France without grandeur stops being France"

These and other famous slogans actively influenced the course of world history. They changed not only the peoples who proclaimed them, believed in them, and died for them, but also the material and spiritual world surrounding those peoples.

This is because the secret to creativity of not just man but of entire nations, according to Buckminster Fuller, is as follow: "You never change things by fighting the existing reality. To change something, build a new model that makes the existing model obsolete."

To sum up the lessons of state-building efforts and the thoughts and ideas of Hetman Pavlo Skoropadskyi, let us formulate the contemporary national idea of Ukraine. To this end, let us first define the cardinal rules or, if you will, the three underlying laws of existence of a modern democracy that reflect Pavlo Skoropadskyi's democratic policy of building the state of Ukraine in 1918.

The first rule (law) of modern democracy is the law of the requisite level of development of the socioeconomic base and political culture of a civil society to ensure the successful operation of institutions of government in a democracy. It states that the essential condition for the existence of a successful democracy is the existence of a critical mass of an affluent middle class, and a level of political culture sufficient to ensure the functioning of the democratic institutions of government; as well as their control and adaptation depending on changes in the internal and external environment surrounding the country.

The second rule (law) of modern democracy is the law of configuration (distribution, checks, and balances) of the governing power- centers in a democracy. It states that real elective status, accountability, and transparency of governing power- centers, as well as the equality of citizens before the law, can be ensured only if the three branches of power – legislative, executive, and judicial – are separated from one another. In addition the maximum amount of internal functions of the state is to be delegated to the lowest possible level of governance.

The third rule (law) of a modern democracy is the law of political stability, continuity, and professionalism by branches of public governance. The law states that an essential condition for political stability in a democracy is the existence of at least two parties founded on a democratic ideology and not leader-centric. They should differ from one another only in terms of their vision of the world (conservative or liberal), but share the self-same common principles of elective status, accountability, and transparency. Each one of the parties should be able (while in parliamentary opposition) to effectively monitor the executive branch of power for as long as the other party is the ruling party.

The preservation of stability and professionalism in public administration must be ensured, first, by a legislatively prescribed system of protection for apolitical professionals from politically appointed superiors who are carriers of institutional memory, expertise, and unchanging traditions of statehood; and, second, by a mass media free from monopolistic influence.

These laws, as well as the historical roots and experience of the Ukrainian people, lay the groundwork for the formulation of my vision of the contemporary national idea of Ukraine in its three dimensions: spiritual, socioeconomic, and state-building, which can be described using the following three mottoes:

1. GOD, FREEDOM, FAMILY, AND UKRAINE—they have always been and will always remain the supreme spiritual values of the Ukrainian People;

2. CULTURE, SCIENCE, LAND, AND OWNERSHIP—fairly distributed between citizens and the state in a balanced manner—will keep Ukraine forever nourished;

3. ELECTIONS, SOCIAL JUSTICE, RULE OF LAW, AND ARMY—they will always protect the rights of Ukrainians to life, freedom, and pursuit of happiness, and will defend the sovereignty and independence of the Ukrainian State..

In my opinion, the combination of these ideas / slogans with the laws formulated above (the "architectural plan") for building a modern European democracy in Ukraine could become the best way of honoring the memory of the great Ukrainian, Hetman.

References:

1. "Apocalypse 375. Collapse of the First Civilizational Project of Eastern Europe". *Dilettante* historical journal, February 2012.
2. Voltaire, *Histoire de Charles XII*, 1731:
3. M. Hrushevskyi, *History of Ukraine – Rus*, Kyiv, 1913 (3rd edition).
4. L. Gumiliov. *From Rus to Russia: Essays on Ethnic History.* Moscow: Ecopros publishers, 1992, p. 87.
5. *History of Mankind. World History.* Fourth volume. Under the general editorship of Dr. G. Helmolt. Complete translation (from German) with significant additions for Russia: select Russian scholars. Fourth volume. *Prosveshchenie* publishers, St. Petersburg, 1896. Recommended by the Main Directorate of Military Education Institutions for military education institutions. Approved by the Teaching Committee of His Imperial Majesty's Own Secretariat at institutions of Empress Maria for fundamental libraries of secondary educational institutions overseen by institutions of Empress Maria.
6. *History of Mankind. World History.* Fifth volume. Under the general editorship of Dr. G. Helmolt. Translation from German with significant additions for Russia: select Russian scholars. *Prosveshchenie* publishers, St. Petersburg, 1896.
7. History of Ukraine in Personalities: Ancient Rus State. Lithuanian-Polish Age / Supervisor of the team of authors: O. V. Rusyna. Kyiv: Ukraine, 2012. pp. 86–91
8. History of Ukraine in Personalities: Ancient Rus State. Lithuanian-Polish Age / Supervisor of the team of authors: O. V. Rusyna. Kyiv: Ukraine, 2012. pp. 86–91)

9. Jordan, *On the Origin and Doings of the Goths*, Moscow, 1960.

10. V. Kliuchevskyi. *Russian History Course*, Lecture 18.

11. O. Kovalevskyi. *Illustrated History of Ukraine from the Ancient Times to Modernity*. Section 10. Third Migration Period. Goths in Ukrainian territory.

12. V. Lypynskyi. *Religion and Church in the History of Ukraine*

13. P. Kraliuk. *Political Portrait of Roman Mstyslavovych*, March 24, 2017, *The Day* newspaper.

14. Karl Marx. *Secret Diplomatic History of the Eighteenth Century*, 1856–1857, Free Press, Sheffield Free Press.

15. V. Petrukhin. *Rus in the 9th – 10th centuries: from the Invitation of Varangians to the Choice of Faith*, Moscow: Forum, Neolith, 2013.

16. Ye. Synytsia. *Wars under Goths: Gothic Heritage in Ukraine Became a Factor of Ideological Strife* Tyzhden.ua, 2012, https://tyzhden.ua/History/44372

17. V. Sidak, T. Ostashko, T. Voronska. *Colonel Petro Bolbochan: Tragedy of the Ukrainian Statesman*, Tempora publishers, Kyiv, 2009

18. P. Skoropadskyi. *Memoirs. Late 1917 – December 1918*. Nash Format publishers, Kyiv, 2016

19. V. Tatishchev. *Collected Works* in 8 volumes, including *Russian History...* Moscow-Leningrad, Nauka publishers, 1962–1979

20. N. Trubetskoy. *On the Ukrainian Problem*, Book 5, Eurasian Chronicle, 1927, Paris

21. O. Sharov, M. B. Shchukin and the "Gothic Problem" // University Archeology. St. Petersburg. pp. 69-75.

22. S. Shelukhin. *Name of Ukraine, with maps*, 1921, Vienna.

23. P. Shtepa. *Muscovy*. Drohobych: Vidrodzhennia publishers, 2012, p. 12

24. Philippe Delorme "Anne de Kiev. Epouse d'Henri Ier, Mere de Philippe Ier. Histoire des Reines de France (Une reine de France venue d'Ukraine)", Pygmalion, Paris, 2015.

25. Timothy Snyder "Russia's Crimea Disconnect", October 10, 2022. Available at: https://snyder.substack.com/p/russias-crimea-disconnect

26. Jacques de Charron "Histoire universelle de toutes nations, et specialement des Gaulois ou François", Paris, 1621.

Ihor Smeshko: The man in the iron mask

In his famous novels about the three musketeers in 17th century France, Alexandre Dumas writes about Louis XIV, a corrupt and despotic French monarch, and his brother, Philippe, a potential challenger to the throne. After an unsuccessful plot to replace Louis XIV with Philippe, the king condemns his brother to a lifetime of imprisonment while wearing an iron mask to hide his identity.

The modern state has substituted more refined methods for that of the iron mask. But the intent is the same – to marginalize and erase the identity of those who are either too principled to bend, or who are perceived as threats to the ruling regime.

Although such abuse of state power is always a tragedy for the individual, it is a greater tragedy for a nation when the "man in the iron mask" is one of its most distinguished, principled and accomplished public officials.

In fact, Ukraine's "Philippe" is the same person who – at two minutes to midnight on the night of Nov. 28, 2004 – saved Ukraine's capital from a replay of China's Tiananmen Square. (See the Jan. 17, 2005 edition of the New York Times).

Who, then, is this "masked man" who – after four repressive years – is re-entering public life and raising his voice against corruption at the highest levels of government?

A distinguished career

Col. General Ihor Smeshko was born in 1955 in Cherkassy oblast. After high school, Smeshko pursued a military-academic career during which he published more than 100 scholarly papers. He went on to earn a doctorate in technical sciences with a specialty in military cybernetics, and a professorship in information and system analysis. In 1992, he joined the newly established Ukrainian Defense Ministry as secretary of its Science Advisory Council, and, later that year, was asked to help set up an intelligence division within the ministry. But before he could begin, he was reassigned to Washington D.C. as defense attache.

Smeshko won many influential friends for Ukraine during his four years in Washington, while earning the admiration of former Soviet and Warsaw Pact diplomatic missions for negotiating the first memorandum on military cooperation between the United States and a former communist state. Ten years later, Smeshko again astounded the diplomatic community by negotiating a similar agreement with the Swiss government – one of only 10 such agreements ever signed by the Swiss.

In 1995, Smeshko was awarded his first general's star, and was recalled to Kyiv to head up the president's committee on intelligence, a position he held for three years. Under his leadership, the committee grew from a "paper" organization to a powerful and influential proponent of reform and professionalism.

Between 2000 and 2002, Smeshko completed a master's degree in military administration as well as a law degree from Kyiv's Shevchenko University.

Building military intelligence

In 1997, Smeshko was appointed director of Ukraine's Military Intelligence Directorate. Once again, he took an organization with no physical assets, no budget, an inadequate legal framework, and a demoralized, intermittently paid staff, and, in 3 years, transformed it into the second most influential intelligence service after the SBU, or State Security Service.

This unprecedented challenge to SBU's preeminence, combined with Smeshko's lobbying for legislation to reorganize and curtail the SBU's residual, KGB-era dominance, earned him powerful enemies. The SBU's counterattacks became especially threatening and intense at the beginning of 2000. The two main protagonists in this secret war were SBU chief Leonid Derkach and military intelligence chief Ihor Smeshko. Although the struggle was largely below the waterline, the visible tip involved control over Ukraine's "dual-use" military technology.

Prior to Smeshko's entry into the world of intelligence and military technology, the SBU, through a network of commercial firms, enjoyed complete monopoly and opaqueness over Ukraine's armament sales. It was not until military intelligence officers were first given the authority to review "end-user" certification in the export of arms that they discovered massive falsification and fraud. The SBU's top brass was enraged at Smeshko's disclosure of highly sensitive and corrupt "affairs" that could have been disastrous to Ukraine's international reputation.

The "final straw" came when Smeshko succeeded in placing the highly effective anti-aircraft Kolchuga system under strict export controls. This precluded its export without the Military Intelligence Directorate's concurrence. After Smeshko was removed as head of military intelligence, the SBU reversed these controls, and embroiled Ukraine in a very damaging global scandal.

In early 2000, the SBU struck back by commencing a sustained, debilitating and humiliating assault on Smeshko, his friends, relatives, and fellow military intelligence officers. They falsely accused him and associates of criminal acts, harassed those closest to him, and spread false rumors that he was "working for Americans." In order to escape rumored assassination, Smeshko resigned as head of MI and took a demotion as defense attache to Switzerland.

Taming the beast

It wasn't until late 2002 that Kuchma urgently recalled Smeshko from Switzerland to help in dampening the exploding Kolchuga scandal that threatened Ukraine's relations with the West.

Appointed SBU chief in April 2003, Smeshko was authorized to reorganize and reform that organization in line with European models. Consistent with Kuchma's call for the "de-KGBization" of the SBU, Smeshko insisted on political independence and on strict adherence to constitutional and statutory norms.

Having spent nine years in various assignments abroad, Smeshko had adequate opportunity to compare Ukraine's security and intelligence services with that of other countries. He recognized that – as long as the SBU retained its core KGB character and mentality – Ukraine's democracy would be at risk; the civil rights of its citizens would be subject to abuse; and Euro-integration would be problematic. However, any reform would inevitably provoke resistance and retaliation.

The first thing Smeshko did, upon being appointed to head up SBU, was to request letters of resignation from its top managers –

something that had not happened in 90 years. Next, he ordered that no documents be destroyed. Thirdly, he moved to increase pay scales and reward professionalism. Having established authority, Smeshko began to boost SBU efficiency through a three-pronged plan:

1. Liquidation of the former KGB's role as a secret political police force, and its subordination to civil state authority. Key to accomplishing this was removal of agents from government agencies;

2. Provide adequate financing of SBU operational costs by eliminating inefficiencies and increasing budgets and compensation; and

3. Reorganization of its internal responsibilities and structure.

As to this last point, Smeshko's plan was to reconstruct it into a "special service" agency responsible for domestic counter-intelligence, protecting Ukraine from foreign espionage, subversion and external interference. In addition, the reformed SBU would focus on complex, large-scale criminal activities that threatened the country's security and constitutional order, such as transnational organized crime; high-level corruption; vote fraud; terrorism; proliferation of weapons of mass destruction; treason and separatism.

Under Smeshko's 15 months of leadership, the SBU demonstrated great progress and proficiency in a variety of cases. Despite considerable opposition, Smeshko completed many reforms. He transferred the foreign intelligence collection function to the newly created Foreign Intelligence Service; and he laid the groundwork for the transference out of military counter-intelligence; and he terminated SBU's influence over government by outlawing the placement of SBU agents in legislative and executive branches.

However, he was removed from office before this work finished.

Yushchenko poisoning

The one fateful event that has hung like a cloud over Smeshko and his family since 2005 has been the poisoning of presidential candidate Yushchenko.

Smeshko's first tragedy is that he agreed to Yushchenko's request to attend dinner at the home of his SBU deputy, Volodymyr Satsiuk, on the evening of Sept. 5, 2004 – the night Yushchenko claims to have been poisoned. His second tragedy is that Yushchenko, despite the sudden onset of severe spinal and head pains a day earlier, chose that dinner as evidence of the "evil, corrupt" regime he was battling. Having staked much of his claim to the presidency on this poisoning, Yushchenko would not find it easy to retract his position without clear evidence against some other party or event.

So much has been written about the poisoning, making it unnecessary to retrace well-trodden trails. Nevertheless, it is key to recognize that no amount of searches and interrogations of Smeshko, and his associates, have ever turned up a scintilla of evidence of any complicity on his part, nor was there ever reason to consider him more than a simple "witness" to one of several poisoning theories.

There are about ten poisoning theories, one of which included the dinner of Sept. 5. Nevertheless, it would be inconceivable for the SBU chief to engage in, or allow, such a risky, high-visibility crime as a political assassination in his presence. Would any top security official in any country in the midst of such a closely watched election have risked such an obvious disclosure of complicity? Many of those who studied the issue closely consider the theory of a Sept. 5 poisoning to be the least likely of the existing ten.

Interestingly, Yushchenko, himself, appears to have had no doubts concerning Smeshko's innocence. Shortly after his return from the clinic in Vienna, he dispatched his aide to reassure Smeshko that he harbored no suspicions towards him. Three months later, Yushchenko officiated at Smeshko's retirement by thanking him for "the cross that he had to bear as head of SBU."

So, how do we explain – four years after the poisoning – the inchoate cloud that still hangs over Smeshko?

One persuasive explanation for a continuing campaign of harassment and vilification is offered by Mykola Obikhod. With a unique insight deriving from work as deputy head in both the prosecutor office and SBU, he believes that all the charges and rumors against Smeshko (including speculation concerning complicity in Yushchenko's poisoning) have all the markings of a high-level, well-organized, procured and politically motivated assault to discredit him, and to preclude him from any future political role.

He believes that the instigators of this campaign are current and former members of the security services who resisted Smeshko's efforts at establishing a competing Military Intelligence Directorate. They continued to vilify Smeshko in his effort to break up SBU's intelligence gathering and reporting monopoly, especially on matters involving high-level corruption, links to international criminal organizations, illegal arms trafficking and the unlawful export of military technology.

Obikhod also believes that the effort to discredit Smeshko may have been orchestrated by colleagues of former SBU chief Derkach. These officials actively concealed Derkach's alleged and reported ties with notorious international criminal kingpins such as Semion Mogilevich.

But the primary reason for the anti-Smeshko campaign – according to Obikhod – has been Smeshko's systemic SBU reform and reorganization, including the loss of its privileged dominance over Ukrainian politics.

Then came revolution

Smeshko refused to take sides in the Orange Revolution. He saw himself as a public servant, loyal to the state, constitutional order, preservation of peace and the physical protection of all citizens. Smeshko expressed his conviction, saying: "not a single child's tear or a drop of an innocent's blood is worth all the intended blessings of 'improving' the world through revolutionary means."

In the winter of 2004, Smeshko played the most difficult role, insisting on SBU neutrality – a position which did not score points with politicians. As popular passions began to rise and the multitudes became nervous over rumors of imminent attempts to forcefully unblock government buildings, General Serhiy Popkov, commander of 15,000 Interior Ministry troops outside the capital, took note of the crowd's restlessness, and sounded the alarm. In the early days of the revolution, his troops were armed, ready and started moving to squash the protestors in Kyiv.

As these events unfolded, Smeshko telephoned Interior Minister Mykola Bilokon in the hopes of preventing a clash. Bilokon said he was responding to imminent threats by protesters to seize government buildings. Bilokon sought assurances from Smeshko that the opposition would not seize the buildings. Smeshko responded by assuming personal responsibility for the safety of government facilities. At two minutes to midnight, the moving armed convoy was ordered to return to its encampment.

Why the mask?

From the very first days of Ukrainian independence, Smeshko devoted all his talents and efforts towards the well-being of his country. He had done so at great personal risk to both life and career. Despite numerous efforts to discredit him, he has never been found guilty of any corrupt or criminal wrongdoing. He had taken on the all-powerful SBU; foiled the criminal schemes of corrupt officials and oligarchs; and saved the state from major international embarrassments and financial losses. He succeeded at every task assigned him, and won for Ukraine the respect and confidence of many of the world's most discerning and influential leaders.

So why has he been marginalized, harassed, humiliated and covered with an iron mask of obscurity? At a time when Ukraine needs leaders with a proven track record of integrity, character, and intellect, how is it possible that a man of Smeshko's stature and capabilities has been buried?

The reason for this lies in his character. Smeshko does not fit well into the political theatre that passes for much of Ukraine's government. He is not an actor, an opportunist or a sycophant. He sees himself as a straight-talking military officer whose prime responsibility is to his country rather than a political party, clan or oligarch. "I was fortunate that my first mentors were front-line officers. They taught me to love and take pride in my fatherland; to preserve the honor of an officer and the trust of my subordinates; and, most of all, to serve and protect my nation and my country."

These words and sentiments sound quaint – almost archaic – in the cynical, pocket-lining atmosphere of Ukrainian politics. Thieves and charlatans have no use for someone who is loyal to a principle.

Smeshko is no ordinary man or public official. His first love is that of an academic and historian. He is currently conducting research for a book on Ukraine's integral role in the development of European civilization. He is also a devout Christian, fluent in English, German and French and – years after his last official position as SBU head – is eagerly sought as a speaker and adviser to business, academic and government institutions.

So we return to our opening questions. Who is this man in the iron mask who has been buried and whose talents squandered at a time of Ukraine's greatest need? And why has this been allowed?

Truly, it seems that in today's Ukraine, such men must be buried and forgotten lest they challenge those now sitting on their uneasy thrones.

By George Woloshyn, "Kyiv Post", Jan. 15, 2010.

Find out more information about the decisive role of Ihor Smeshko with developments of the Orange Revolution in the article «How Top Spies in Ukraine Changed the Nation»s Path» by C.J. Chivers, "New York Times", Jan. 17, 2005.

Full version of the article is available at: https://www.nytimes.com/2005/01/17/world/europe/how-top-spies-in-ukraine-changed-the-nations-path.html